Parental Emotional Abuse

Its Impact on Adulthood

Page 132 - Line 4 - (o- have
have

Parental Emotional Abuse

Its Impact on Adulthood

Barbara Stuart, MEd PhD

Parental Emotional Abuse

Its Impact on Adulthood

~~~~~~~~~~

Copyright © 2014 B. Stuart, MEd PhD
Faith Restoration Ministries International
www.frministry.org
ISBN-13: 978-1495487262

Contents

Lo, children are an heritage of the

Lord: and the fruit of the womb is

his reward

[Psalm 127:3]

Preface

The incidence of childhood abuse is real and should not be ignored as though it is not important. There are adults who are still working through a parent's insults, poor treatment and disregard for him or her. Those who were able to comfort themselves and move on had to purpose in their hearts that there is nothing they can do about the past.

Nevertheless, for some adults who grew up attached to the memories, it is extremely difficult to extricate themselves from the past.

Since every child expects unconditional love from parents which is normal for all infants, when this is lacking it leaves them with images in their minds and empty spaces of emotional beehives. Many husbands abuse their wives; others are alcoholics; and some are addicted to harmful substances: all casualties of parental emotional abuses.

Maybe you are wondering why those persons cannot shake the past. The assumption could only be an unforgiving heart which will lock anyone behind an emotional fire wall.

If parents tried to be more considerate about the feelings of their children, they would make every effort to see that their childhood is pleasant, even if they cannot afford expensive toys and other incidental amenities. There are managers, who routinely abuse their subordinates,[1] who are only trying to do a day's work to support their families.

What is most important to a child's life is sincere constant love. This is a commodity which should come easily from every parent to a child.

In the formative years when the child is most vulnerable and trusting, he needs the mother's love who should be more caring even if dad is not present.

---

[1] See Employee Emotional Abuse: *Oppressive Working Environments*, obtainable @ www.frministry.org

Since more households are headed by single parents usually mothers, it would not be harsh in saying that they, should be more thoughtful and loving to their children; it is the least they can give to them.

Children do not see gray lines even when parents are bickering. What they need are parents; but unfortunately, many of them did not have parents who truly loved them.

Some parents who did not show love to their children were <u>ignorant</u> of their needs, <u>too preoccupied</u> with their own life, or just <u>did not care</u> because they were cruel, brutal, harsh and insensitive to those needs and the feelings of the children. Others were <u>rigid</u> with discipline, <u>neglectful</u> and openly displayed <u>rejection</u>, with which some adults are still trying to cope.

The stories in this book will paint pictures of parental abuses, the memories of which have followed some into adulthood impeding them in their social and emotional life.

It is during adulthood that many children express themselves in an attempt to rid themselves of painful past abuses which they suffered. There are broken relationships, divorces and many other situations which affect them such as alcoholism and drug addiction.

Parental Emotional Abuse: *Its Impact on Adulthood* comprise of four parts: **Part I:** *The Family*, **Part II:** *Life-Changing Events which affect the Family Structure*, **Part III:** *Childhood Emotional Abuses*, **Part IV:** *The Effect of Childhood Emotional Abuse in Adulthood*, **Part V:** *Healing from Childhood Emotional Abuses.*

Part I

The Family

———————————

God sets the solitary in families

Psalms 68:6a

He takes care of the lonely

1

An Overview of Family Life

According to Craig (1996) "Parental and family influences are just one element in the larger process of socialization…the lifelong process by which individuals learn to become members of a social group, whether a family, a community, or a tribe" (p.95). Therefore, if we are to believe and accept this thought, children born into a family should be treated with love and appreciation. They should not be abused in any way or form; but this is not always the case or the ideal.

It also means that each parent has the godly and moral responsibility to help that child understand and learn the art of socialization relating to values, beliefs, self-control, culture, roles and customs. However, if the home environment is a place of disorder, fightings and emotional inconsistencies these are what the child will adapt and act out when he is away from home.

Parents must understand that they are the ones who make the choice to bring children into their lives. Children did not come into the world all by themselves, they came out of families.

Families are formed by a man and a woman who make the decision to become one flesh. It is from the union of a couple [a man and a woman] whether married or unmarried that children are born.

For this reason it is necessary to include a section on family life since children are abused by someone who lives in the residence. There can be no contradiction that many parents are involved in the abuse of children either directly at their hands or by someone who visits the home. The abuse does not necessarily have to be physical but can be verbal and or emotional.

The home should be the safest place for every child, but it is not always so because of abuses and various forms of situations which cause chaos discontent, and so many other distresses.

Children should see expressions of appreciation in the home, since this is the first place of learning for them. The behaviour displayed by the parents is what the children will imitate and follow.

Typically, in each home there are boundaries and unwritten or invisible rules, which guide each member of the family concerning what is required from each one. If there were no boundaries, the system would deteriorate inviting all manner of destructive elements into the home.

In any case, boundaries must be clear, and understood by each member of the group. There should not be any uncertainty about the meaning of a rule so that children can follow accordingly.

One of the major problems in the home occurs when there are mixed messages and a child violates a rule causing a parent to issue discipline which might be injurious to him emotionally or physically.

Every parent has desires and hopes for a child. Nevertheless, despite the well-meaning plans there are many situations, which will cause the framework of the family structure to fracture.

Those may include abuses of all kinds either to the child or to a parent. Including is the visible intake of various types of drugs, alcohol, pornography, destructive games and many other factors which cause unnecessary pain. It is from those situations which create an atmosphere of restlessness.

In addition, there are times when death takes away a breadwinner and this might leave the family financially impoverished. Many people can relate to incidents such as this, yet they were able to overcome the sudden loss, financial distress, and other factors to raise successful emotionally healthy children.

However, when any of those circumstances occur, it does not only affect the immediate family but also, the extended family members, community and the society. The reason is that most children take out their frustration at school or in the community causing havoc and destruction in their paths.

Therefore, when problems arise they must be managed in a controlled manner and in an environment which is conducive for effective communication and dialogue. In some situations, the family may need outside help from either an objective family member, pastor, doctor, or a therapist. At times having someone else listen to problems works wonders if the disputants are willing to talk and are open to suggestions.

The family relate through communication of its goals, values, rules, and the way each member manages conflicts. Children learn from parents and this is why the system must be set up with guidelines which they will follow either from examples or direct teaching. Each member should feel included and important as the other.

In every situation, the communication must be effective. This means that each person will think of the emotional effect of using the wrong words, attitude and so many other influences, which can result in painful consequences. The family is important and everything must be done to keep it intact and strong.

2

The Structure of the Family

As a system the family cannot function effectively on its own. Therefore, members within the framework must work together for harmony and balance. It is a complex system which requires the support of each member since no one can successfully function without the support of the other. Where one finds a family of two or three generations the children seem to be in a more socially, morally and spiritually controlled environment. This is the reason why culture plays a significant role in the rearing of children.

Although the family system may seem well organized, there are times when there are problems in the structure. Those problems often affect the system either positively or negatively. With the aid of an experienced objective individual, even a family member who understands the development of children and family problems, those situations can be dealt with without suffering adverse setbacks.

Clearly, unity and respect are vital for the successful stability of any family. Each member must function by assuming his or her role effectively for strength and resilience, especially in the times of challenging circumstances.

It is during life-changing events the family will either strengthen as a unit or disintegrate and fall apart. Furthermore, each member knows that despite his position in the family, he is no greater than the whole. He is only one part of the entire family [system].

Goldenberg & Goldenberg (1996) reported that, "Murray Bowen, the developer of family systems theory, conceptualizes the family as an emotional unit, a network of interlocking relationships, best understood when analyzed within a multigenerational or historical framework" (p.145).

The writers observed that "Rather than functioning as autonomous psychological entities, individual family members are inextricably tied in thinking, feeling, and behaviour to the family relationship system" (p.147). Borrowing the adage "all for one and one for all" seems very applicable with this point in describing the family and its function as a unit, yet individually. Agreeably, the members of a typical family do interact as being dependent on each other.

Craig (1996) stated that it is the "family, which exerts tremendous influence on the kind of person the child becomes and on her place in society" p.93. The writer further noted that "the way people interact in families has an enormous impact on development" p.93.

Obviously, harmony is essential along with confidence, loyalty and the expressions of love so that each one feels that he is as important as the other member. Despite this important factor, the effect of the influence the family has on children will be the deciding factor on how they behave and the types of experience they will take into their adulthood.

For example, if the child does not receive constructive feedback from parents to encourage him to achieve his goals in life, this will be a setback for him. This makes one ask the questions "Do parents really know the impact negative treatment to their children have on their adulthood?" "Are they aware of the hurts and emotional distresses they cause their children to endure when they label them with names which may seem applicable because of the mistakes made?"

Each child is different and will only excel with the natural abilities with which he was born. One child may aspire to greater intellectual heights because of innate intelligent attributes, but all may not be the same.

Still, despite its impressive impact in society, the family has become one of the most endangered systems due to the changes in its structure and methods for parenting. Nevertheless, the family life is still and will always be a fundamental influence in the social system.

Currently, families face various kinds of challenges which just a few generations ago could not disrupt the structure as they are now doing.

Seemingly, there is an ongoing diabolical revolutionary force whose aim is to change the concept of what use to be normal family life for the abnormal and in some situations, utterly obnoxious and absolutely detestable model.

The attempt is to radically transform the biblical framework of godly moral love, unity, one man and one woman to something which is rebellious and ungodly. Even recent publications of Bibles are depicting the new morality which is of a destructive nature and completely alien from what used to be wholesome appropriate behaviours. The opposition and obstruction of God's plan for marriage will certainly have an effect on His model for family life.

Indeed, the family is under societal siege which is imposing all kinds of despicable and offensive theories for the rearing of children, and for a sustainable and lasting marital relationship.

Paul, in his writings Ephesians 5:20-6:1-4, focussed on the family teaching how to live and interact with one another. There should be selflessness, and seeking the good for the other person's welfare. Each member of the family should feel safe and wanted in the home. No one should feel inferior.

The main idea is that when children are born into a family, they should be happy and well protected. Unfortunately, because of various problems some of which are environmental, some homes have become war zones. Children live in fear of abuse either to themselves or to a parent.

In some situations, parents use drugs in the presence of a child who might grow up thinking this is the way to feel happy and solve problems. Furthermore, when divorce, adultery, or physical abuses infiltrate the family structure they cause all kinds of emotional pain, and psychological problems to children and the injured spouse in the relationship. Those conditions only undermine the structure of the family system when social germs enter the home. Those elements are destructive mechanisms, empowered by spiritual forces, which usually contaminate the atmosphere.

The media is the main source through television, pornography, the internet, and some music. Indeed, everyone is free to make choices; but those choices are often selfish and by people who are egotistic. When social germs infiltrate the family structure, they create new values because in some cases there is a quid pro quo attitude.

Take for instance when one spouse commits adultery, the other might feel inclined to do the same and sometimes it happens. Consequently, there is no concern for the welfare of the children as morals decline and values deteriorate. Since it is from the home environment where children gain their first socialization experience, it is therefore important for them to obtain the right teachings which are normal and proper.

Even if parents choose to do what they believe is right for them, they should not visit their sick beliefs on to their children. Those children are impressionable and will emulate what they see, and hear to be right from parents whom they trust and love.

Parents often have the most impact on a child's future endeavours. Some children even choose the same interests such as political party, select careers and professions they believe will impress their parents.

Regardless of what society represents and promotes for normal family life, the Christian interpretation of the family structure will remain intact even if only a few follows; it cannot be torn down and demolished by proponents of what is wrong.

3

Description of the Family System

A typical family formation can be considered as a structured system with subsystems for proper function and effective communication. The subsystem consists "as parts of the overall system assigned to carry out particular functions or processes within the system as a whole" Goldenberg & Goldenberg (1996), p.44.

In such a setting there a hierarchical structure organized for clear understanding of what is expected from each member. In a healthy setting there are boundaries, which tell each person what is acceptable behaviour, rules, values, and principles. Some expectations are prescribed while others are implied for each to follow by example.

Seemingly, whatever happens in a child's life or even as an adult might be traced to the family structure and the methods used to resolve conflicts. Another could be the organization of the family system.

For example, one family maybe open where individuals are free to express themselves while in another setting, only certain ones have this privilege.

In some situations, dad is the only one who makes and alters rules in the home and children are completely excluded for making any decisions even in choosing friends, or careers. Dad has exclusive rights to discipline, to direct and control each person even mom who might have no authority to express herself or for instructing the children.

In another construction the family may be enmeshed where everything even sexual abuse is kept private. Often dad will caution the children that *"whatever happens in here stays in here...do not speak to anyone about our business...we take care of our own."*

In such a setting conflicts are ignored and difficulties are not discussed. Although they live under a cloud of dysfunction and deceit, they all seem comfortable shrouded by fear of making a mistake or the outside world intruding on their life.

4

Communication

The family is a system with subsystems mentioned earlier in this section. It is through the medium of communication that subsystems identify boundaries, rules, and roles. Therefore, each member must be clear about what is expected of him or her. In some situations verbal do not match the body language and this will create conflict and cause distress.

For these reasons communication must not be vague or ambiguous to cause misunderstanding because it is a vital component for maintaining the system and keeping it functioning effectively. Therefore, the *type*, *timing*, and *quality* of the communication must be relevant for accomplishing harmony among members.

Family members relate to each other through the communication of its goals, values, rules, and the way each member manages conflicts. Children learn from parents from the rules and guidelines which they will follow either from examples or direct teaching. Each member should feel included and important as the other.

Despite this, the success of communication in the family depends on the relationship of family members.

Each person must be respectful to the other because "the clarity of the subsystem boundaries is far more significant in the effectiveness of family functioning than the composition of the family subsystems" Goldenberg & Goldenberg (1996) p.45.

Therefore, when disagreements occur between members of the family it might be the result of poor communication patterns or misunderstandings to the meaning of a message.

Communication is the normal way we interact with one another. It is a two-way process, whereby we send out and receive information. However, it is not complete unless the recipient understands the message. To understand means that there will be some type of response from the recipient. This goes for both verbal and non-verbal communication.

Clearly, communication will either be effective or ineffective. The reason is that we cannot successfully communicate until we learn to *listen, interpret, reflect, explain,* and *ask* questions in order to gain understanding of what the other person is saying or said.

Nevertheless in some families, a child is not allowed to ask questions; and only hears "*do as you are told*." It is likely that there will be confusion and problems in this type of home. One could infer that the setting is fertile for any kinds of abuses to members of the family especially to a child who is impressionable and who will make mistakes.

Any violation of boundaries may prove critical which will make a child become fearful and subdued not knowing what the outcome will be. Even if he knows the result it may be harsh and this will intensify his fears. It is vital that boundaries are clearly explained to a child so that he at least knows what is expected of him.

One of the major changes in communication which will take place in the family is with an adolescent who is still sensitive and trying to make sense of the world. In some homes there are two or three generations present and this can create various types of communication crises whereby the teen believes the parent or grandparent is "old-fashioned and does not know anything." That individual does not want to hear from adults, but rather pays heed to peers.

Craig (1996) pointed out that, "With adolescence a time of significant and often dramatic change, the family as a social system also changes, as does intergenerational communication." She further added that, "these changes…can be particularly difficult in single-parent families" (p.441).

This is logical especially when the single parent is the provider with no other income coming into the home. The child may resent the hours the parent is away from home earning a living.

It is at such times the parent ought to explain the "facts of life" to the child so he or she understands the value of providing for the family even though it means being away from home for long hours. The child needs to know the implications for not providing for the family and the impact of poverty.

One child told a mother "I used to sit in class wondering if we will have food to eat when I got home." These are some the concerns children have but sometimes cannot communicate to the parent. Therefore, parents must communicate to a child who can at least grasp an understanding of the reasons for parental absences, and long hours of working, and even about unfavourable situations.

The proper interaction of family members is vital whereby each person understands each other in order to respond effectively to differences with respect and consideration.

What does it means to communicate?

Many families communicate to each other with disrespect and poor exchange which often cause conflicts. Sometimes the message is heard, but not understood by the recipients. There are times when a parent needs to be explicit when there are others' around so that individuals know without doubt for whom the message was intended. Effective communication occur if each individual takes time to listen, interpret, and understand rather than react impulsively.

Consistency: say what you mean and mean what you say

Paying attention: being present and not inattentive. You cannot be reading and listening at the same time when your child needs your attention.

Inclusivity: although members of the family maybe in one place together, there are times when certain individuals are excluded from family conversation. This will create discouragement. If the conversation is meant for one or a few then ask the one not required there to excuse himself or herself or, you go somewhere else or wait for another appropriate time.

Being wanted: each person should have a sense of being loved, wanted and included in the family. Children should not feel that there are gender differences among siblings which occur in some families.

Fairness: parents should not show differences with the manner in which children are handled. There must be consideration for the feelings of each child. It is wrong to show high regard for one and not the other by openly insulting the one you do not esteem. This will cause friction among them and emotional pain to the recipient.

Differences in Communication Styles

There are differences in the style and manner in which each person communicates. For this reason parents must be careful how they handle each child. Moreover, one might be an introvert and submissive who likes quietness, while another is just the opposite and may take offense to a sharp rebuke, unlike the former.

A mother and child were having a conversation when the she asked, *"How am I doing as a mother?"* The response was *"I do not like when you shout at me."* This information changed the attitude of the mother and the way she communicated with the child after that conversation. Children are sensitive and they too, have likes and dislikes. They should not be penalized for speaking their minds in a controlled respectful manner.

There are four identifiable communication styles

a. The Aggressive Child: a parent may have a child who is forceful and sometimes hostile towards other siblings. He might seek the parent's attention because he wants to be heard when there is a problem. Nevertheless, he might be the type of person who does not listen, always interrupts in order to dominate or to achieve his personal goals. This behaviour will cause strain on the family because that child can be selfish who does not care how he gets what he wants so long as he is satisfied.

There will be times when he gets bossy with demands and will do anything to monopolize a conversation. That child will place guilt on the parent and use criticisms, shouting, and anger to communicate his feelings. He will be a major factor for chaos and hostilities in the family. This is where the patience and time of the parent will be greatly needed to help this child so that he is able to cope in the real world.

b. The Passive Child: this child tends to be very submissive and will obey even when it hurts in order to please the parent or even another sibling. The parent will see the difference with one who is aggressive and the submissive child because they are opposites in comparison to their behaviour patterns. The passive child always let others take the lead to prevent confusion or any form of disagreement.

Parents must be very careful in this situation especially if another child in the home is aggressive. It will be easier to attend to the bossy disobedient child to prevent fights more than the one who does not make demands to keep the peace.

Another point is that the passive child may be the one who is treated unfairly because he or she is dependable and will be given more tasks than another. If parents do not pay attention to the personalities and communication skills of their children, many will leave home broken and disappointed about their childhood experience.

c. The Assertive Child: parents of the fifties may consider a child with this type of communication style to be boisterous and rude. Yet, in reality they are not. Being assertive shows confidence, self-assuredness and optimism maybe regarding life and what the individual believes. Despite their self-confident attitude those children can be very sensitive to the feelings of others especially those who cannot defend themselves. An older child who is assertive will respectfully say to a parent "Dad, do not be so hard on Jonnie." He is not ordering the parent around; instead he is showing concern for a younger sibling whom the father may be treating unfairly.

d. The Passive Aggressive Child: this is really a combination of the passive and aggressive communication styles. This child uses guile, with nice words to get to the heart of a parent who might not realize he or she is being used until later. The child is manipulative in a subtle way to achieve his goal.

All parents will experience any or all of the styles or a combination depending on the circumstances and situation a child faces. It would not be wrong to say that any child will communicate with a parent depending on the parent's own style of communication. The advice to parents is to be vigilant, and to use the style which most suits the child's personality and the situation.

Ineffective Communication

Charlee arrived home from school with a scowl on her face. It was the aftermath of an interaction with a girl on the bus who called her a name. Mom had a day off from work and was watching her favourite soap opera. She acknowledged Charlee when she greeted her but did not notice the bump on her forehead.

Charlee: Mom a girl struck me on my face because I told her to mind her own business.

Mom: Uhuh. Go take a nap still watching the television and did not look up. Charlee was a very assertive child and was not willing to give in, but insisted to get her mother's attention.

Charlee: Mom, you are not listening.

Mother: Oh, yes I am.

Charlee: No you are not! What did I say? You did not even look up as she stormed out of the room crying...

A scene as reported above will make the teen become isolated with anger. He or she will not express feelings and may reach the point where he or she does not care and may not show interest in family affairs or even school.

The sad thing about this is that some parents are so pre-occupied with themselves that they do not notice changes in their children.

In such a situation it is possible that distancing might follow as communication continues to breakdown. The teen will no longer want to share hurts or concerns with a parent who is cold and insensitive.

If parents do not show interest they are sending a message to a child without a word being spoken. The teen will become angry if parents are inconsiderate and do not show interest in his or her life, and especially in school work.

When this happens the teen will not trust parents and will disrespect them. Although the child is responding according to the communication she receives, it is the parent's responsibility to correct the child by taking time to guide and teach with proper examples which the she can follow.

Charlee's mother should have stopped what she was doing or watching and paid attention. It is evident that she was not listening because her interest was in what was in front of her. She could not respond with the correct response of showing emotions and physically hold and console her daughter who was physically and emotionally hurting.

The mother heard the words the daughter spoke, but did not hear her emotions to reflect and empathize with her. Moreover, body language is most effective when it comes to communication. In this case, there was no response and this made the daughter escape the cold and insensitive atmosphere.

Communicating with your Teen

1. *Model good behaviour:* Do not send out mixed messages, they are confusing.
2. *Be responsible:* Accept blame when you are at fault. Claim your weaknesses and be honest when doing so.
3. *Allow personal growth and development*: We all make mistakes, so will your teen.
4. *Do not criticize:* When there are mistakes be kind, acknowledge and reinforce efforts. Do not point out the negatives in the presence of others. Choose the right time and place.
5. *Decisions:* Allow the teen to make decisions, and include him or her in your family discussions and plans. For example, do not act arbitrarily on your own with the expectation that your teen does not have a life.
6. *Ignoring:* Take time to know your teen and for your teen to know you.
7. *Pretend:* Do not pretend that you were perfect when you were a teen.
8. *Putting Down:* Do not put down your child. Look for areas of improvement and give recognition.
9. *Labeling and Name*-calling: One of the mistakes parents make is to insult a child by describing him or her in a derogatory manner to cause distress and embarrassment.

Barriers to Effective Communication

Inattentiveness is a deterrent to effective communication. It restricts open discussion and meaningful exchange. We can see in the scene above that the mother, though she said she was listening was obviously physically present, but not emotionally.

Disrespect: parents must avoid disrespecting each other in the presence of their children with the use of hurtful words. Since the home is the first stage of learning for children, they will imitate their parent's negative behaviours. Furthermore, they should not engage in verbal assaults because they usually end up in physical violence.

Taking Sides: parents must be fair when dealing with conflicts and not take sides by inciting one child against the other. One parent should not use a child against another parent. Teens act out because of the stresses of life on their young age. They have not lived yet; they are only in the process of living. Parents should give them *space* and *opportunity* to express themselves. They should show understanding, patience, and *sincere* love.

Overly Critical: criticizing a child for wrong doing is not enough. What the child needs to know is how to do better next time. Too often parents spend more time being critical rather than reinforcing the efforts a child makes.

Unclear Instructions: parents must be clear when giving instructions to children for each one to understand. They should avoid the use of innuendos and be specific about their desires.

Deception: parents often pretend they love each child equally, when this is not true. Children do know the difference. They know if they are loved and whether there are differences with siblings.

Insensitivity: some parents lack true sincere feelings for their children, and will create hostilities among siblings.

5

Communicating in the Family

The family system is the first organizational social group which humanity has known. The members share cultures, beliefs, and various other factors which influence the structure. It is in the family system where the development of "intricate overt and covert forms of communication" are conceived with "elaborate ways of negotiating and problem solving that permit various tasks to be performed effectively" Goldenberg & Goldenberg (1996), p.3. Through the interactions in the family individuals learn to share ideas, opinions, likes and dislikes as they communicate feelings with each other.

In a safe environment there will be no need for fear and openness of expression is encouraged. Children will have the freedom of sharing grievances from school especially if either of them faces bullying. Despite the social organization of the family, there are times when some hurts from the outside is kept hidden by children because there is no one to care about their distresses.

One *person* reported that she had no one at home to share her problems when as a child she was bullied at church by the pastor. Instead she kept all the pains and distresses on the inside and only spoke about them much later in life.

When the home is a place of bondage and abuses children suffer and carry their emotional pains into adulthood. Evidently, it is clear to see that the *person* mentioned lived in a home where expressions were not encouraged and communication was mainly in the form of emotional abuses.

In a family where there is free expression for feelings, there will be a collective understanding among members relating to the world around them, rules, procedures, self-expressions, instructions and discipline.

Each member will be encouraged to communicate in an atmosphere free of ridicule and embarrassment, things which cause distress whether within the home or from outside.

In the case of the *person* mentioned earlier there was no such opportunity for expression. The individual stated that if she had reported the matter to the caregiver she would be the one to receive blame.

Nevertheless, the typical healthy family unit is *strong, confident, sincere*; and fortified with *love, respect, rules, roles, order,* and *morality*. Well, this is what used to be. In a dysfunctional family setting, if family problems were traced, one might find that the communication system was emotionally defective, confused, closed, mixed or just did not exist.

The communication system might have been a weak inadequate structure with nothing substantial to endure severe economic and other life changing situations which often affect everyone.

Since those circumstances are often inevitable due to fluctuations in national political and other conditions, the aim of effective communication between parent and child is "to help the adolescent emerge from the last stage of childhood ready to assume adult responsibilities" (Craig, 1996, p.441).

The parent and child communication is most vital at such a time. Therefore it is the responsibility of the parent to help the child understand those realities and teach them how to cope when they appear.

The problem with this point is that inexperienced individuals who became parents at an early age, maybe in their teens head many single-parent homes. How can a parent in such a position communicate effectively to an impressionable teen?

It is in such settings that some children rebel and parents become angry with shouting and various forms of abuses. Those abuses are critical to the emotional health of the child who cannot understand the ideals of the parent who is only trying to guide and direct him or her.

With a difficult teenager the situation may become extremely complex because the parent is trying to be kind, while simultaneously taking care of herself, and even other younger ones.

The weight of the burden may become overwhelming and cause the parent to become angry with harsh painful words to the teen. The communication structure will break down and feelings will be hurt on both sides.

Conflicts will occur and unless the parent is able to confront without abuse, there will be confusion and much misunderstanding in the communication patterns.

Craig (1996) stated, "Generally, early adolescence is more conflict laden than later adolescence" p.441. Therefore when parents do not communicate effectively, there is the tendency for the child to want to leave home early, while the parent may be permissive in an effort to keep the family intact.

Another important point is for parents to communicate to their children and teach them the types of behaviour they expect from them.

The emphasis here then is for young parents to seek out some form of parenting support in order to teach them how to communicate with their children.

Frequently when problems occur in the home it is due to ineffective communication causing misunderstandings and various forms of complications resulting in dysfunction.

Parents must set boundaries and ensure that each member of the family follows accordingly. They explain, ask questions, and teach children according to the maturity and readiness.

Furthermore, parents must set examples for communicating before their children in terms of dealing with conflict, failures and problems. These must be communicated through direct teaching and modeling.

In terms of communication it is not enough for parents to verbalize everything. Rather, there must be examples which the children will emulate by parents' performance and attitudes.

Children will learn how to love each other and to share with others from the home. This will teach them socialization so that when they are away from home they will know how to conduct themselves. Evidently, children "must be raised in a responsive social environment if they are to show optimal developmental outcome" (Craig 1996, p.204).

Undoubtedly, the onus is on the parents to communicate values which will help their children build wholesome character and make them responsible citizens in the family, community, and nation.

Effective communication also means that parents must explain the purpose for discipline. They should not keep scores on their children's misconduct, but correct them immediately indicating what is acceptable and what is not.

Moreover, parents should make it easy for the child to communicate problems and hurts to them instead of going outside of the parameters of the family.

When this happens, it shows weakness in the structure, which might also be unstable. There should be family discourse when they are together to talk about affairs and problems which are troubling to their peace of mind.

Referring to effective communication this is not always by words but by behaviour patterns. If the parent lives a life which is questionable; for example, having several partners, the taking of drugs and over indulgence in alcohol, it will send the wrong message to the children.

Finally, the format for effective communicating in the home begins with one person giving a message to another who will listen, interpret, understand and return with feedback. Communication is not complete until the message is received, acted upon and returned with a response.

Each person must be willing to listen, ask questions, and provide explanations to retain the integrity of the family union.

It is from the feedback received that changes are made for misunderstandings and miscommunications. Keep in mind that nothing is achieved with shouting and anger. Everyone must be willing to accept differences and this includes parents and children and vice versa.

Since no two persons are the same parents must treat each child according to his or her personality.

Avoid name-calling and using negatives to describe children. When there is misunderstanding, confront with "Did I hear you say…," instead of "You, said…." Do not try to change your child into your personality.

Everyone should learn to accept differences in communication, and sometimes make sacrifice by changing opinions which are contrary or which cause confusion to others. Always think of the feelings of the next person and not only your own.

In terms of family life, spend as much time as possible with each other. Do things together and talk with one another. Children should feel safe to express themselves and their feelings without fear of reproach.

There are times parents expect all the children to be the same, but this does not happen in any family. This would be a negative attitude which the children will find confusing and cause distress to them.

Effective communication is vital for the successful existence of the family structure. This means that the parent must assume responsibility to instil in the child from early who is in charge and what rules are meant to be.

The rules and roles must be thoroughly explained to each child with fairness and in love. Shouting and harshness will not solve problems and misunderstandings.

6

Family Conflicts

Disagreements in the family environment may be the cause for abuses in childhood especially if there is alcoholism or drug abuse which will rob the family of needed financial support. Alcoholism may be the cause for unemployment if the provider becomes careless and loses employment. This may leave one parent working to provide for the family while the other lives off the earnings coming into the home. This will cause arguments and frequent quarrels which will affect the children in the home. It is the concern for a secure home and threat of separation which will make a child become sad and discouraged.

From that discouragement he or she may lash out at a parent who is already over-whelmed with anxieties to respond in anger, thus making life even more difficult for the child. Conflicts may also be the result of one parent loving one child and shows this openly with no regard concerning how the behaviour will affect the rest of the members in the home.

This lack of concern will create an opportunity for conflicts to develop. In another situation it could be that there are members [maybe young adults] who are unemployed and sitting around all day doing nothing, and this can be the greatest cause for family conflicts. Family conflicts are part of life, and when they occur it could be the cause of communication problems.

Family Conflicts

Effective communication in the home is a significant element which will keep the family together and in harmony with one another. Nevertheless, the major problem with communication occurs when it is ignored or misunderstood. How often do we hear "Oh I did not mean it that way." "Sorry for the misunderstanding." It could also mean that a parent spoke to a child at the wrong time or place and this can result in problems in the family. When misunderstandings occur they cause conflicts which are disagreements between at least two persons.

Unmistakably, if the home is dysfunctional the style of communication might be indirect, unclear, inaccurate, and so forth. Where these factors are evident it means that there will be conflicts which might disturb the entire family system depending on the nature, timing, place, and persons who are involved.

However, if the system is healthy whereby each person is able to confidently express concerns, conflicts can be resolved effectively. Moreover, conflicts might just be timely to repair and settle problems which have been developing for a long time.

In contrast, "Dysfunctional families do not permit individuality and members fail to develop a sense of self-worth. Parents with low self-esteem communicate poorly and contribute to feelings of low self-esteem" (Goldenberg & Goldenberg (1996), p.139.

Undoubtedly, children living in a dysfunctional home do not have the opportunity to express themselves. It could be that parents do not spend time to listen because they are concerned about their own relationship and do not consider the needs of the children. Undeniably, children living in such an atmosphere will develop low self-esteem because they are not allowed to speak about problems.

Instead they will conceal their feelings which may cause them emotional misery, as they grow into maturity. These are the situations which occur in childhood and appear in adult relationships.

One feature about conflicts is that they have a systematic nature because there are steps that lead to a conflict. For example, an *event* occurs, leading to the *perception* of its occurrence as review and evaluation take place through *cognitive processing* with questions such as "why," "what" and so forth.

Next, the *reaction* or *response* to the event occurs when the *affective* takes over which is expressed in *emotions*. It is after appraisal of the event that we often react or respond in an effort to find out the <u>reason</u> for a situation, or to <u>alleviate</u> the pressures of emotional hurts. Finally, those two areas – the *cognitive* and the *affective*: thoughts and emotions are communicated into **behaviours**, which may or may not lead to conflict.

However, the unique factor about conflict is that of itself, it is innocuous. Conflict only becomes destructive when handled improperly. The unfortunate point concerning childhood hurtful events is that the child may not pay attention to the emotional response and will repress his feelings. Later in adulthood it may only take one painful event to unearth the past causing distress and anguish.

In the situation of a parent and child the parent may take out his or her anger on a child who had nothing to do with his or her past. Yet the parent who is uncontrollable will strike the child in anger and chase him away.

Another point is that parents and children often are at conflict against each other because of age differences, changes in culture, trend, and a myriad of other things, which they could have handled differently, if they were conscious of their communication styles.

Influences on Family Conflicts

Conflicts can be the cause of incomplete or faulty *communication* fueled by *culture* inherited from one generation to successive descendants.

The style and type of communication may also be affected by defective morals which are socially destructive. These originate from the *media*, *pornography* and the *internet* which influence the communication process in many homes of today.

The diagram below gives an example of the factors of communication which affect the family structure either positively or negatively. These are the <u>culture</u> in which the child was born, the <u>media</u> and <u>society</u>, including the *church* and *school*.

Parents have the responsibility to decide which code of ethical standards they will adopt to guide their children.

Table 1

Influences on Family Conflicts

Morals are based on three particular standards

Culture	Media	Society
The culture in which a child is born has a strong effect on his or her personality. However, not all cultural values and traditions are suitable for each generation. The ease with which people are able to travel will bring changes. This includes inter-racial marital relationships which will certainly affect cultural beliefs, morals, and patterns of behaviour. Each family sets its own rules and values which it finds suitable for the members.	Un-supervised Television programs, destructive music genre, and the Internet with its free-flow of information are direct influences on the family which will affect its communication style and patterns of behaviour. Many parents are not able to control what the children watch, read or listen to when they are absent from the home. There is also pornographic literature which family members bring into the home, or children acquire from friends, etc.	It would not be fitting to blame the **society** for all the ills of family life. However, it has a direct influence on its structure and style of behaviour. There are activists with their personal values who will go to extremes to indoctrinate the population with what they consider to be right. The **church** also is a factor with the various types of beliefs and doctrines some of which might be contrary, but family members uphold them in the home. The **school** has its own ideologies administered through teachers and government agents.

Adapted by B. Stuart, 2014

Some Causes for Problems in the Home

There are many situations, which will result in conflicts. Usually, the most important and provocative problem is miscommunication among family members: spouse/spouse, sibling/sibling, parent/child/children.

Until we take time to *listen* to hear what each is saying and to be empathetic there will always be turmoil and conflicts causing disagreements and poor relationships in the home.

Frequently, spouses divorce each other when there was no need for doing so. They become selfish and forget the children in the marriage.

Every family has differences which will keep the communication channel open if they took time to discuss and examine the causes for problems. The handling of those conflicts will result in either win/win outcomes or destructive situations.

The Causes Include but not limited to the following situations

a. Unfair demands towards one another
   i. Parent/parent; parent/child
   ii. Sibling/parent; sibling/sibling

b. Unrealistic expectations

c. Undue influence [*excessive demands*] parent/child – fearful

d. Mixed messages resulting in misunderstanding

e. Poor communication skills

f. Poor parenting skills. Some parents are immature and need teaching and support

g. Setting poor examples before children by telling them one thing, but displaying another

h. Domestic abuse– witnessed by children will hurt them emotionally or they might visit this behaviour on their own spouses

i.   Over permissiveness. There are parents who will use gifts to win a child's affection or to play one parent against the over

j.   Discipline - too much or non-existent

k.   Parental abuse either emotionally or physically. Some children end up in the ER or die at the hands of an angry cruel parent

l.   Financial problems – unemployment, over-spending, gambling

m. Children being left to the *elements in society* – adult television programs, and the internet

n.   Lack of Family Values: *principles, standards, codes, beliefs, ethics, morals*

o.   Lack of respect for one another

   i.   parent/parent;

   ii. parent/child;

   iii. sibling/parent;

   iv. sibling/sibling

p   Poor interpersonal skills. Being abrupt, selfish and aggressive

q.   Lack of effective role models – parent/parent

r.   Failure to deal with issues by allowing problems to develop into open arguments, tension and discord in the home

s.   *Ambiguous instructions*: parents who are not clear and specific with their instructions

t. *Deception*: parents who pretend to love each child equally, when this is not true.

u. *Failure* to admit to weaknesses and faults.

v. *Unreliability*: you do not carry out plans on time, or keep promises.

w. *Insensitivity*: conflict will occur if parents show lack of interest in their children

7

Managing Conflicts

Problems are unavoidable, and everyone faces something which causes distress or concern on a daily basis. Therefore, family problems are not new as we can see with the very first family at the beginning of the world. When problems arise, it is time to check the system to find out what is wrong; where are the weaknesses, and decide how those weaknesses are going to be fixed in a non-threatening environment. There must be trust and respect for one another; commitment to carry out the plans for correction; and a desire to retain a harmonious and pleasant atmosphere.

Since problems do not always give warning as to their occurrence when it happens, this should not be a time for creating further problems by abusing – verbally, and physically, blaming someone, running away, avoiding or pretending that those problems do not exist.

Anger, abuse, hostilities, and animosities are no solutions for dealing with problems. There are many ways which people use to manage conflicting situations. However the points following will assist every parent in the management of family disagreements.

Collaboration – Family Conference

Collaboration really calls for teamwork where everyone is willing to co-operate to reach the same goal. It is a group effort where each relies on the other for support.

- We do this by joining with each other to discuss and find out what has caused the problem. Each person must listen to the other and wait for the completion of a statement.

- Make the atmosphere relaxed so that each can discuss the best solution from the presenting options.

- There will be no competitiveness or manipulation for territorial positions because each person knows his or her role.

- There should be no jealousy among the members.

Getting Answers

1. Ask open-ended questions and avoid asking closed questions with "yes" and "no" responses. How can I help you? "How can we work together to resolve this situation?" Rather than "can I help you?" or "You are the cause for the problem facing us." Remember that the family is a unit and what affects one member will affect each person in the system.

2. Brainstorm for options, and do not criticize.

3. Make sure that everyone understands each question.

4. Give time for the other party to think and respond.

5. Design your questions so that they are not ambiguous or intimidating.

6. Leave room for clarification and explanations.

7. Probe gently with the use of open-ended questions: Why did you? How do you feel? When? What? How? Why? Encourage the person to describe what

happened, and show genuine interest with body language and emotions. These will be more effective than being accusative and blaming.

8. Be sensitive to the other person's feelings.

Encourage Participation

1. Be flexible, reflective, empathetic and open-minded.

2. Encourage many ideas, but do not criticize.

3. Allow each person to speak giving equal time to each person with respect.

4. Be patient as you encourage silence.

5. Discuss various ways for meeting needs.

6. Devise options for solving the problem.

Seek for Solutions

If there is a fault in the communication process in any group/family/organization, there will be problems. The error when issues arise is that individuals have the tendency to overlook those situations, rather than deal with them immediately. Problems result in conflicts, which may lead to a break in the relationship. Every family member needs proper order for the system to be functional in order to survive. Conflicts of themselves are harmless. What makes them offensive is the way individuals process difficult situations to either bring about the right results or cause conflicts to escalate.

Changing Your Behaviour Patterns

Thoughts can become powerful intra-psychic struggles resulting from incompatibilities which affect our needs, desires, and life. Those are the situations which create the framework for conflict in families making members become angry with each other.

For example, if dad who is the sole provider becomes unemployed, it will be the summation of his thoughts about unemployment and the inability to provide his family which will give him the stimulus to act negatively causing emotional outbursts of anger, conflicting clashes and hostilities.

In such a situation the family should give support by encouraging him, and thanking him for his contribution in the past. They should not yield to the outbursts, but influence him to remain confident that he will obtain another job.

Clearly, then the emotional response given to an event is the result of the cognitive evaluations of the situation which cause an individual to react in ways not always acceptable.

Consequently, conflict is a combination of cognitive, affective and behavioural modes which each person uses to make sense of the world and events which occur and sometimes change plans.

Setting Goals

Every family has goals of which each member should be aware. Everyone should know what is required and the rules of the family. Parents consciously plan how they will bring up their children and the desires they have for them. Despite the fact that tragedies will sometimes upset the plans, this should not prevent anyone from setting goals. What is most important is that the goals are necessary, realistic, and reachable.

Traditional Values

Every family has traditions which will either propel them forward or hold them back. Those traditions may be sacred to one person, while to the next generation they are not necessary, but who sees the need for development and change. For example, children may not like the traditions of their parents. They may spend time debating why the traditions should remain, while the children will point out how unnecessary they are to their own personal livelihood, family and interests. Nevertheless, with proper management those differences can be resolved in an amicable manner.

Feedback Mechanism

There are rules, which serve to guide and lead the family members concerning expectations, boundaries, roles, values, and so on. Feedback is a control response system, which will guide and direct the parents concerning what works and what does not. It will also reveal who is abiding by rules and those who are being objectionable.

Feedback is necessary because unless the parents know what is happening in the home, the system will break down as we have seen all across the globe. If there is no meaningful feedback mechanism, the family will eventually fall apart. This takes place when husbands walk away, and children leave home in anger before time.

The family without a feedback mechanism will certainly suffer losses in a myriad of ways. There will be disappointment and emotional traumatic situations affecting everyone connected and those indirectly connected, such as society and the next generation.

Listening – Being Present

One of the weaknesses in the communication system occurs when people are not willing to listen to each other. This issue has caused many problems in all types of interpersonal relationships. Effective listening is an essential factor in the process of communication. There must be reflection, summarizing, clarification, and explanation. Also, the speaker must be congruent, otherwise the content and purpose of the message will be misunderstood.

In the typical home, we have the father and mother and they each have significant roles mandated by God towards each other and for the family. The roles incorporate emotional, spiritual and social demonstrated between members of the family.

It is the parents' responsibility to provide social, spiritual, and practical training for their children. They should give the basics so that the child has some knowledge of right and wrong before going out to associate with others.

When the home life is unhealthy because of rebellion, the children take their hostilities away from the home, to church, to school and in the neighbourhood. One can assume that many times when a child misbehaves the root cause comes from a home where there is no guidance from adults.

Children must be taught to listen and act upon what they heard. Therefore, they must learn when to speak and when to listen.

We cannot hear each other unless we listen to each other. It means that parents will take time to *discuss*, *re-phrase*, *reflect*, and *attend* with *respect* so that each child understands the message.

Children learn from parents, therefore, parents have a significant role in demonstrating proper communication skills to their children.

When communication is open and flows easily, this gives opportunity for *co-operation*, *attentiveness*, *trust*, *confidence* in expressing oneself, and *respect* for each other.

1. We cannot solve problems unless we learn to listen to each other. We listen with our senses – *ears*, and *body* with *gestures*, *nods*, *facial expressions*, *posture*, and *eye contact*. Therefore, we must move beyond just hearing words. Instead, we must *reflect* upon what we hear and then ask the right questions.

2. We listen with our emotions so that the individual knows that we are concentrating. There must be *empathy*, *concern*, and *sensitivity* to the needs of others.

3. The person must want to hear what the other is saying before any engagement into the activity of listening will happen.

4. Both parents and children must learn to give their undivided attention to one another. This means being fully aware of body language as well as verbal.

Poor Listening Skills will cause Conflicts

Has anyone ever said to you, "You are not listening? What do you think the person meant? Were you annoyed, knowing you were not attentive? The truth is that you were present, but were *not* listening to what was said.

Your response might be "I heard you," but did you *really* hear? Maybe you were miles away or your mind was on something else. Children know when parents are listening to them because they stop what they are doing and pay attention.

The parent who does not pay attention to a child is communicating a message of "I do not care about you."

Whether it is spoken or not, this is the message the child will hear. We do not only speak words, but the unspoken body language reveals the truth by the way we respond more than words alone will do.

Incongruence: saying one thing while meaning something else will cause disagreement in family relationships resulting into conflicts.

8

Angry Parents

There are parents who seem unaware concerning the effect of their anger which sometimes make their children become fearful. Anger is an emotion, which disturbs everyone at various times during a day. The expression may not always be volatile, but anger can be dangerous when it gets out of hand.

Every person can identify when the emotion is imminent, and has the ability to recognize the signals. Despite all this, parents do not always try to control the onset of anger. Nothing is wrong with parents expressing their feelings, but there must be consideration for the effect this will have on the children.

Many parents use anger as an instrument to obtain compliance from their children whether they are disobedient or not. Another reason could be that parents see themselves in their children who act out the way they did when they were their age. It could also be the result of a childhood memory of abuse which might cause a parent to be angry with a child.

Maybe the parent is fearful of expressing true feelings because of shame, embarrassment, or displeasing the child who might not approve of the behaviour. Instead the parent uses anger for self-gratification because it makes him feel better.

It becomes destructive when a parent disciplines a child in anger. In some of those cases even babies are hurt or killed because a parent became angry with crying or such like.

Parental anger can also be from verbal or physical assault after an abusive encounter with the other parent. The danger is that if a parent uses anger to relate to his children, it might one day be the cause of the child's death which has happened in so many situations.

Some children may not lose their lives, but they may be taken from home by the State, or sent to live with a relative. No matter what the situation might be; parents who terrify their children with anger are doing them an injustice, and are indeed cruel and abusive.

Frustration

Frustration is usually the result of unmet needs, disappointments, failures and other situations which affect the life of the individual. Individuals who did not complete high school but became parents at an early age might take out their frustration on the child whom they see as the object of their lack of accomplishments. They might blame the child and emotionally cause abuse which will affect the child in a variety of ways.

He might think that he is a bother and might be just as angry with the parent or turn the anger on the inside and later in adulthood display it on the wrong persons.

The cause for some internal anger could be that the individual is frustrated about what he or she wants to be; but society, family, friends, or any other situation impedes the fulfillment of a secret desire.

The frustration occurs because the individual experience obstructions and hindrance. Other reasons for frustration could be personal values, public outburst concerning certain choices, and many other situations which cause discomfort.

All those circumstances can be the result of internalized anger. Internal anger may lead to bitterness and will become destructive and unmanageable. One of the reasons why people internalize anger could be that they do not want to face themselves honestly.

Unforgiveness

If there is anger in the heart, then there is also the spirit of unforgiveness. This spirit will corrode the soul because the individual no longer trusts in God and does not care about his relationship with Him. He no longer listens to the Holy Spirit, but responds to what his flesh demands. Those could be retaliation, resentment, vengeance and so on.

An unforgiving heart will separate the individual from God [Matthew 6:14-15]. That heart harbours malice, hatred, and deceit. It is difficult to reason with such a person because of the hardness of the heart. The unforgiving person can be vindictive and merciless.

When unforgiveness is present, healing of the hurt cannot take place. It is as if a brick wall is standing between the individual and his healing. That wall is supported by anger each time the memory of a painful incident surfaces.

The unforgiving person can be very cruel and he seeks any and every opportunity to get even with someone. It does not matter who feels the heat of his anger or the venom, which proceeds from his behaviour.

9

Anger Management

Anger is a normal human emotion which everyone experienced at some time or other in life. The effect can range from mild irritation to intense fury and rage. Feelings of anger actually produce physical changes in the body such as increased heart rate, raised blood pressure, and the sudden rush of adrenaline. For some people, it does not take much to make them angry.

An outburst could be caused by anything from a friend's annoying behaviour to worries about personal problems or memories of a troubling life event. When handled in a positive way, anger can help people take positive actions to fight injustices.

On the other hand, anger can lead to violence and injury when it becomes destructive. Many children are hurt with words or physical attacks from the result of a parent's anger.

Some ways to deal with Anger

Ignore – walk away

Some people choose to ignore or bottle up anger, but this approach may actually cause more harm because the root problem was never addressed. Instead, try to manage anger so it can become a more positive emotion.

Relax

Breathe deeply from your diaphragm (your belly, not your chest) and slowly repeat a calming word or phrase like "take it easy." Think of a pleasant experience and happier times.

Think positively

Remind yourself that everyone is not against you, but rather you are just experiencing some unpleasant events of daily life. [See Philippians 4:8].

Problem-solve

Identify the specific problem that is causing the anger and approach it even if the problem does not have a quick solution.

Communicate with others

Angry people tend to jump to conclusions. Slow down and think carefully about what you want to say.

Listen

Listen carefully to what the other person is saying. Know that constructive criticism will help you.

Manage stress

Make sure to set aside personal time to deal with the daily stresses of life which often comes with work and family. Ideas include:

- Listening to music
- House work
- Walking
- Meditating
- Talking about your feelings with someone you trust.

Deal with your Emotions

Emotions such as stress, sadness, or fear may cause someone to feel angry. In the case of a child he should tell a parent, teacher, or other trusted adult if he:

- Regularly feels irritable, or in a bad mood
- Becomes angry which seem to last for days at a time
- sometimes feels like hurting the self or someone else

It is possible that those feelings and the accompanying behaviours could be signs of depression which is a sickness needing professional attention.

10

Changes in the Family System

The constant instabilities in society relating to governmental administrations and political unrests, including the whimsical nature of people, the family system has been re-defined with new structures to comply with the desires of the masses rather than adhering to what is sensible. In most situations, family life is no longer the once well-organized unit it was a few generations ago.

In some homes, children are often on their own for long hours which could be because of national economic upheavals, when a parent faces foreclosure, loss of employment, and various forms of financial distresses. These are some of the inconsistent circumstances, which in some cases are inevitable.

Every parent wants to support the family in the best way he or she is able to do; but with the economical fluctuations everywhere, it becomes a difficult possibility. Situations such as these will make parents become angry when they cannot adequately provide for their family, as life gets stressful for them.

Still, one of the mistakes parents make is to think only about their needs and desires and forget that children are an important part of the family structure. A wife may say to her husband "I can do without you, leave," and the husband vice versa. Whoever is at fault fails to realize that since there are children in the home and decisions can no longer be about themselves. They need to include the children and make plans based on what is best for the entire family.

The reason is that the structure of the family system includes inter-related subsystems, which must work together. No one system is independent of the other because they each need the other for proper functioning and effectiveness. Each member is important and needful to maintain homeostasis. Therefore, when there is a fracture in the plans everyone suffers. It leaves children to take care of themselves; while a parent takes on two or three jobs to support and keep the family together especially after a divorce or death of a parent. It is like a vicious circle with each situation impinging on the other.

These are some of the situations which cause the change in the framework of family life. However, one cannot always blame life-changing circumstances and economical unrests for the deterioration of family life.

Another important point is that some children do not know about morals and godly disciplines because there is no one to teach them or even to point them into the right direction.

Parents become engulfed with cares such as job security, health, and financial concerns. Each day as the children seek for answers and the meaning to life, things continue to crumble around them. They no longer have parents or even know them unless they are sick or the authorities are at the door.

The decline in morality and new order for family life prompted Ekstrom & Roberto (1992), to make following prominent point affirming that, "Family life and traditional, religious values were once the glue that naturally held people together. They were the roots in our society."

The writers further stated, "In pursuing personal goals and material wealth, families and groups in our culture are not united as meaningfully as they could be" (p.4).

Obviously, these statements are evidence of the breakdown of the framework of the family as values slowly disappear through greed and the quest for more personal fulfillment at the expense of moral and religious values. People consider these more important than a cohesive family life.

Undoubtedly, consistency in family life seems no longer a goal because the entire structure is bombarded constantly with a mosaic array of sophisticated devices, *disguised* in the cellophane of delusion, *decorated* with the tactics and strategies of devious forces, and *supported* by the stimulus of worldly wisdom.

We cannot minimize the fact that there is a well-organized influence at the root of the breakdown of family life. The force works systematically to intrude on its plan with well-defined designs to bring complete destruction even if this was not the intention. However, the end result shows with the increase in crimes in society among unsupervised youth.

The conclusion is that the family structure has changed, and it will take a decisive effort to restructure and reaffirm the values which once held families together. If children have a firm foundation especially during the formative years, there is hope that they will grow up with the correct attitudes which are sociable and acceptable towards life and people. They will not respond with negative behaviours to manage conflicts and other life-events, which they will face as they develop.

Every family should do all in its power to stay

together for a better and secure life.

Family is still one of the greatest social

arrangements in the world.

Do not allow insensitive forces who have no desire

for unity and morality to destroy it.

11

Characteristics of the Family System

Social scientists recognize the family as a system with three subsystems: parent-parent, parent-child, and siblings. Other smaller subsystems include extended relations. Within the immediate family system, rules are established to "enable each member to learn what is permitted or expected of him or her as well as others in family transactions" Goldenberg & Goldenberg, (1991) p.36.

Clearly, if each member knows, understands, and accepts those rules there will be harmony in the home. Those rules govern how each member interacts with the other and what behaviours are acceptable in the system which can be healthy or unhealthy.

The Healthy Family System

In a healthy setting, roles are clearly defined, rules are explained, and power is shared although the parents take the leading roles, and the children follow accordingly with the understanding of what each has to do. The primary goal is to maintain balance within the system in order to survive.

In addition, the power lines are identified through an effective communication system to maintain order. Besides, in such a setting, the communication style is open, there is respect for each other with effective feedback, love, laughter, and all the dynamics for free flow of expressions that lead to homeostasis in the system.

It is the rules that clarify the kinds of behaviours that are accepted among family members. Therefore, when parents breach the very rules which they set, the children are confused, frustrated and disappointed. Those children will be anxious because they are not sure what to do, or what to believe.

The assumption here is that when parents violate the very rules they set before their children with behaviours that are emotionally destructive, then those children lose respect for them.

It is very disturbing to hear parents using foul language to their children, and the children echoing equally to them. It is a very despicable behaviour since it sets the standard for dealing with conflicts in the home and the child's personal life. If those kinds of behaviour are what the child learns at home when he goes to school he will not show respect for authority because he does not know how.

Therefore, violation of family rules by parents and any destructive conduct will affect the attitudes and behaviours of children, and this comes through the communication system, even without a spoken word.

Unhealthy Family System

One evidence of an unhealthy family system occurs when one parent tries to influence a child against the other parent or use the child as a referee, this is called triangulation.

This triangulation could also be in the event of a child misbehaving and the mother calls upon the father to intervene. If he is not present or refuses, she may call on another member who might take on the responsibility to persuade the troublesome child to behave (Goldenberg & Goldenberg, 1996).

In an unhealthy situation the stability of the family becomes critical and members will be anxious about the outcome from a problem. It does not matter whether the cause of a problem is from external or internal source, it will create distress which everyone will experience.

The problem could be sudden death of a parent, a child's behaviour at school, the loss of a job or any unexpected circumstance to cause stress. In any case, triangulation will work successfully depending on the nature of a problem and how it is resolved. Another very important point is that a vulnerable child in the system may become "triangulated into parental conflict" (Goldenberg & Goldenberg, 1996, p.153).

Take for example, *Sonya*. She reported that whenever time her parents' disagreed, either one would use her to transmit messages to the other who is present.

Jack also said that even though his mother was present, his father would say to him, "Tell your mother to…" which often left him very distressed and angry on the inside, but he could not express the anger because dad was lenient towards him while mom was strict.

The unhealthy family structure leaves no room for creativity and exploration. Children have to be in order and only speak when spoken to because "Dad says so." Boundaries are unclear, but any violation might result in severe punishment.

Moreover, good efforts at school and proper behaviour are not acknowledged since the understanding is what is expected of a child. Children are discouraged to bring friends home and they are kept in strict order because it is the expectation of a parent.

In some unhealthy homes it is possible to find that there is evidence of incest kept well hidden so that the "secret" does not go out. Children must remain inside and visitors are met at the door.

The unhealthy home is a dysfunctional place which harbours deceit with coercion from family members with the intention to abide by cultural traditions and selfish rules to keep order.

Members of that type of home are abused in all the areas mentioned in this book despite the efforts sometimes to take the family to church. This can be misinterpreted as morally good, but when investigated the family is often in bondage.

An unhealthy family setting is no place for growth and development. Seemingly the one who is wielding the rod takes advantage of individual member's freedom for selfish and other unnecessary reasons.

Other Elements of the Unhealthy System

1. Evidence of alcoholism and drug addiction

2. Multiple fathers/mothers causing jealousies among siblings

3. Favouritism is prevalent depending on which father gives the most support

4. Poverty even if this is only borderline

5. Incest, which is often a well-kept secret by family members

6. Various forms of abusive behaviours

7. Children are ridiculed and mocked

8. Pornography and adult movies be shown in the open with children watching

9. It would not be unusual to hear of multiple felonious offenses, may be by the father who might be incarcerated

10. Children are left unattended with no supervision

11. The traffic in such a home is heavy with all kinds of intruders/visitors

12. Lack of social graces

13. Disrespect for order and authority

14. Parenting skills are more injurious than helpful

15. Children are without discipline, morals, and proper guidance

12

Parenting

Sarason & Sarason (1996), acknowledged that, "Parents affect their children's development from the moment of conception, through the genes they contribute, the parental environment, and the physical and psychological environment in which the children grow up" p.565. Therefore, each parent has the responsibility to rear the children in an orderly manner: the effect of which will contribute to the family and those with whom they interact.

When children become disorderly and unmanageable it would not be wrong to look to the kind of parenting skills and the environment in which the child is living. We learn from our environment and adapt to the stimuli which influence the way we conduct ourselves under any given situation.

The child who learns self-control and respect for others will not viciously attack another or try to bully his way to get what he wants. However, if this is the custom he has seen in his family where dad shouts and demands what he wants, certainly the child emulates and displays similar behaviours when confronted or he needs something.

Assumingly, children who are bullies learn from their parents who have set faulty examples of socialization before them. It is what they *know*, were *born* into, *grew* up with, and *displayed* before them on a daily basis.

Bullies do not come out from the dust nor do they come from in the air like the common cold germs. They are coming from parents who did not exhibit the right techniques for conflict management and emotional control on their children.

Moreover, when parents abuse each other and display aggressive behaviours in the presence of their children, they are transferring destructive styles of behaviour for managing disputes. Those behaviours will eventually become the method the children will use when they have their own problems.

What many parents do not understand is that child abuse does not always have to be physical.

Rather, child abuse can be emotional and or psychological which can have a damaging effect on the child and might even affect him in adulthood.

Admittedly, parenting did not come with a manual, but abuse of any kind should not be an excuse to issue personal hurts in angry expressions on an innocent child.

Young children are influenced by what they see and hear more than what is deliberately taught to them.

The parent may say to the child "do not hit your sister," but if he sees his dad hits his mother, this is what he will replicate and not what the mother or father forbids him to do.

Environmental values will always influence the way an individual learns and behaves.

Therefore, when the child sees repeated abuses at home, he will certainly adapt those examples and will repeat them at any given moment in the presence or absence of the parent.

13

Modeling Acceptable Behaviours

Although there are many negative forces behind the immorality in society, nevertheless, frequently parents themselves are at fault. Furthermore, when parents have disputes with each other, they should not involve the children to cause them pain and heartache. It is sad to note, that very often the disputing parents do not think about the consequences of their actions in the home. In addition, some parents do not consider the effect their behaviours have on their children.

Moreover, any immoral action by a member in the home or by a close relative, viewed by children can affect the moral structure of the family system. Young children copy what they see, while older children may confront the offender [parent] to obtain answers for inappropriate behaviours. Those children often have to deal with confusion and irritation, and they may become depressed.

If proper examples are not set before children, they will follow the behaviours that they have seen in their immediate environment as the right thing to do. This means that if the children are aware that mom or dad is behaving in a manner that is unusual with someone of the opposite sex, this will make them unhappy and disappointed. Those children will become frustrated because they no longer know what to believe.

Furthermore, when the marriage breaks down, it is easy for them to think that it is their fault that mom and dad do not love each other anymore. It may seem inconceivable, but some parents do view children as obstacles, when they decide to carry out their schemes to cheat on one another.

Apparently, many parents fail to realize that children are very impressionable, and they take things very seriously. Therefore, if one parent uses a child against the other parent, this can be detrimental with lasting effects on that child. The misunderstanding of the situation will follow even into adulthood.

Unmistakably, infidelity has placed a dent into the family structure making marriages very tenuous. Well, since marriages are so weak making them unstable, I wonder if parents should prepare children that one day, mom, and dad might divorce if they do not love each other anymore. This thought may sound extreme, but rational.

Nevertheless, maybe parents should prepare children for the inevitable in marriages due to its uncertainty in this age. The sad thought is that when parents *know* that the stability of the marriage is uncertain, yet they lie to children, and on one another. They blame each other to present a reasonable front before the children. How long can this go on? Eventually those children are able to arrive at a conclusion with an understanding of the facts, as they grow older.

Positive Examples

God expects parents to set clear and clean examples before their children so that they can learn and adopt the right qualities that will lead them to make the right choices when faced with decisions.

Here are some techniques for setting effective examples before children. Parents must display these fundamental qualities to their children from birth, and most certainly during the formative years. They are crucial in the life of a child during his development.

1. Parents must set godly principles in the home
2. There should be godly and moral standards through demonstration and teaching

3. Family altar should be an integral part of the weekly routine

4. Parents should hold regular family conferences

5. Parents must express sincere love towards each child

6. Parents must show constant respect for each other and for children

7. Parents must show kindness towards each other

8. Parents must express gentleness towards each other

9. Parents must take time to listen with emotions

10. Parents must support, encourage, and validate their children

11. Parents must show concern for each other

12. Parents must always show forgiveness

13. Parents must show sensitivity, warmth and appreciation

14. Parents must complement each other often

When these qualities are present and demonstrated consistently before children, parents are building an environment, saturated with peace, joy, and well-being.

Negative Examples

Children's perception of problems in the home will often make them feel sorrow, grief, and disappointment. They can experience those feelings when their parents' divorce each other, or when they cross the line and cheat on one another. When this happens, many children become depressed, inattentive in school, and sometimes they will display unusual behavioural problems both in school and at home.

One does not need to argue that a survey is hardly required to accept the fact that a firm and stable marriage builds a strong family. This includes children who will possess a high degree of self-concept, moral dignity, and a solid spiritual foundation. Again, it is from this structure that a strong community and nation emerge.

If the child grows up hearing remarks of failure, and criticisms, intimidation and such like he or she will be discouraged. Furthermore, children in such a setting grow up with an inferiority complex. They believe that they will not amount to anything good, and this faulty teaching leads them down the destructive aisle of failure and despair.

Parents should avoid name-calling, excessive and inappropriate discipline, labeling, intimidation, anger, and shouting at the child.

Some Negative Behaviours include the following

1. Insulting the child

2. Name calling

3. Threatening with violence of austere punishment

4. Verbal abuse

5. Lack of support

6. Intimidation

7. Ignoring the child

8. Failure to acknowledge accomplishments in a child

9. Comparing one child to the other with insults to the one not liked

10. Lack of acceptance of a child

11. Violation of the child's personality difference

12. Telling the child he or she is unattractive or good-looking

13. Constant anger towards the child

14

Teaching by Examples

Proverbs 22:6 *"Train up a child in the way he should go: and when he is old, he will not depart from it."* The passage is very clear showing that when parents invest their children, this will yield untold dividends as they grow and mature. The child needs love, nurture, and discipline and this must be with wisdom and understanding.

The training of a child involves teaching them godliness and moral principles, which will cause them to acknowledge God and having respect for authority.

Including with the training is teaching the management of emotional situations and conflicts, which affects each individual daily. They need to know how to deal with anger and how to behave when things do not go right in their lives.

Parents must also treat each child with due respect and according to the child's personality and natural gifts. Furthermore, the parent must teach the child to avoid the tendency to allow peer pressure to allure them into wrong behaviours [Proverbs 1:1-10].

Children need examples from the parents, which will guide them to make the right decisions when the parents are absent. If the parents make the effort and do the right thing, their children will indeed, take their training into adulthood.

Parents should not consider training of their children to be a burden, and therefore leave them to outsiders or grandparents to do.

The responsibility for training is a God-given one and He will require accountability from the parents. Furthermore, when parents invest in the training of their children, they will not have regrets later in life.

Nonetheless, it would be difficult for children to learn without positive examples. Therefore, if parents are emotionally and spiritually stable, they will impart valuable knowledge to them. This is where the behaviour of the minister is critical. If he disrespects his wife and does not spend time training his children, he is leaving them to be respond to all kinds of vices. Some pastors' children have become addicts and involved in situations, which are immoral and ungodly.

The Scripture rightly states, *By their fruits you shall know them* [Matthew 7:20]. What would be the point of telling a child to adopt healthy living if the parent is a smoker, an abuser or adulterer, behaviours which are easily learned in those developing years?

Moreover, sons are likely to follow in the footsteps of a father: while daughters will adopt the mother's behaviours and attitudes toward life and life-changing circumstances.

Consequently, if parents do not live honestly and uprightly, they cannot expect their children to behave any differently towards laws, authority and discipline. Whatever parents sow in the lives of their children, they shall later reap the harvest.

Discipline

It is important for parents to teach discipline to guide their children in the right path for life. This is achievable only if they train their children in effective communication to listen and ask questions politely, to respect authority, and to obey instructions. All children need order in their lives, and there are three important learning environments exposed to children from birth to adolescence. <u>The first place is in the home</u>, <u>the second will be in church</u> – or place of religious education, and third <u>the school</u>. When we put the three environments together, they create a learning organization in which children receive education, either vicariously or directly.

Avoid Unrealistic Expectations

There are parents who place unrealistic expectations on their children. This causes them to become uninterested and sometimes they fail even to try. If when they do their best and a parent condemns or criticizes by demanding what they cannot give, this will send a child into the arms of someone who will appreciate him or her. It does not matter from where the help comes. That child will feel wanted when someone shows interest in his or her efforts.

If parents practice correct effective examples of behaviours before children, evidently they will emulate by repeating those actions. Therefore, when parents fight in the presence of their children, they are teaching them a negative way for handling disagreements.

It is the responsibility of parents to teach the principles of social morals to their children, by demonstrating love and compassion before them. When children do not receive proper training in the home, they will accept behaviours they see in others, which could be wrong and might lead them into danger.

Moreover, the parents' responsibility also includes teaching their children to fear God and to do the things which are right. Parents should not depend on a religious setting to teach their children values of morality and godliness. If they display forgiveness, love, and show kindness before the children, this will help them in relating to those persons they will meet in school, church, or where they go for social interaction.

Since the home is the first learning environment for teaching in the child's developing years, it is vital that he receives the right training to help him mature into a successful, moral, and godly person.

Parents should not *provoke* their Children

Parents provoke Children in the following ways:

Nagging: parents do get infuriated when children do not carry out chores in a timely manner or they keep their room untidy.

Discouraging: children become discouraged if the parents constantly fight with each other or when they do not keep promises.

Use of harsh words: some parents are very inconsiderate, and will use words which are hurtful to describe a child. It is even worse when the child is compared with others.

Belittling: when a parent demeans a child and puts him down when he has done his best to excel, this will make him sad and unhappy. Belittling a child is extremely degrading and cruel.

Anger: when parents approach their children in anger, this is outrageous and dreadful. They use anger so that children behave and comply with rules. There are times when even the mother is fearful and has to submit because dad is always angry.

If the parent has to resort to anger to relate to the family, then there will surely be disrespect, coarse language, and various other situations to cause distress and emotional horror.

Disrespect: although some parents do not think that their children require respect, they do. Children are people and have the same emotional needs as do adults.

While the needs of the children may not be enormous, yet parents must recognize that they too have feelings and can be embarrassed. Saying "please," "sorry" and "thank you," will go a long way from a parent to a child.

Comparing one child with another: some parents are very insensitive towards one child. Usually, they display this behaviour as an insult calling the child stupid, and other ugly names to teach the unloved child a lesson in an attempt to try harder at school.

The problem with this behaviour is that parents must realize that a child in this position may be emotionally scarred for life.

It is wrong to put down one child while the other is elevated because of good grades in school. Everyone does not have the same level of intelligence, nor does everyone have the same aspirations.

Physical, mental, emotional, and spiritual abuses: there are various kinds of abuses which many children experience or witness in the home.

It matters not how the abuse is demonstrated, it is wrong for children to have those scenes in their collection of childhood experience.

Abuses are painful for a child to witness and even worse when he or she is the victim whatever form the abuse takes.

Biblical Principles to Follow

Colossians 3:20

"Children, obey (your) parents in all things: for this is well pleasing unto the Lord."

Obey*:* to hear, give heed, and yield. To obey further means to listen attentively, respond, and submit without reservation. Consequently, the child hears, responds, and obeys. However, the child does not only hear with the *ears*, but also with the *eyes* and with the *emotions*.

If the parent is unkind and uses insulting words, this is what the child responds to, and nothing else will have any meaning to him. No gifts, nice house or clothes will be of any real significance.

Well pleasing*:* this means agreeable, acceptable, and pleasing not only to the *kind* parent but also to teachers and other authority persons. The child who is constantly being abused will take a stand whether *mentally* or through *attitudes* to respond negatively to the parent's insults and humiliation.

There are times when a parent will say that a child has "sass or lip," but the behaviour is in response to what the child receives.

The Scripture states, *Therefore all things whatsoever ye would that men should do to you, do ye even so to them: for this is the law and the prophets* [Matthew 7:12]. This is commonsense and fair. If the parent desires the child to be obedient, it is his or her responsibility to set the stage for this to take place.

Some parents believe that since they provide the necessities of life, the child **must** comply with any and everything they desire, and **must** accept any form of treatment. *Wrong*, hear what Paul said to parents.

Colossians 3:21

"Fathers, provoke not your children to (anger), lest they be discouraged."

To Provoke

This happens when a parent annoys, frustrates and irritates a child with *name-calling*, *put-down*, *ridicule*, *insults* and the use of *demeaning words*. There are parents who will cause a child to become enraged because of unfair treatment specifically, when it is through the medium of favouritism.

Some parents use comparisons either with another sibling or family member. *"Why can't you be like…?" "You will not amount to anything." "You had better improve otherwise, I will…" "You are a disgrace to this family."* Some children are provoked to the point of taking drugs, joining gangs, leaving home early and so on.

To be Discouraged

Children become extremely discouraged when parents use harsh words, nagging, and show disdain to their efforts. Anyone who has experienced discouragement will attest to the fact that it is a feeling of despair, gloom, sadness, and constant worry. The child who is humiliated or neglected by a parent will be discouraged.

Proverbs 18:14 reads, The spirit of a man will sustain his infirmity; but a wounded spirit who can bear? Discouragement leads to depression and helplessness.

Influences on Family Life
Society

Balswick & Morland (1990) in their reference to crime and juvenile delinquency, noted that, "All societies have regulations that prohibit behavior considered destructive of the social order; they require conduct which will maintain that order" p.69. Despite this statement, there are parents who are facing difficulties rearing their children because the society has invented principles gleaned from ingenious ideologists who pose as the supreme knowledge and authority in opposition to what is right. Some of those ideologies are for the most part alien to the Biblical principles used over time for a Christ-centered home where the fear of God is present, and children learn respect for the self, others, property, the law and authority figures.

One reason why the family system has weakened is that sincere fidelity in marriage has become unconvincing, even in the church community. For instance, if members in the church are guilty of adultery, then this behaviour will affect the sacred institution of marriage on both sides of the fence, that is, both in and out of the church. Some of those behaviours have ended up in divorce.

Moreover, some people are quite comfortable to consider divorce as the *only* means to heal a sick marriage. Statistics [*not available*] have reported that there are as many or even more divorces coming out of the church in comparison to society. If this is true, then it is time for the church and society to wake up.

It is inescapable, but if the institution of marriage, which is the main foundation for effective family life has failed, then this is clear evidence that the strength of the family structure is very insecure.

Additionally, today, we hear of alternate life-style, same-sex marriages, gender change, and trial marriage, and some will tell you outright that marriage is not necessary because it is only a piece of paper. Each one of those ideas is indeed a diseased concept spewed from the mouths of people who are selfish, godless and arrogant.

Points to Ponder

1. With the effect of societal influences, what is the solution to those new ideologies which have invaded the minds of people anesthetizing and lulling them to sleep?

2. How can we take back our families held captives in those types of iron-grid theoretical manacles?
3. Does the world's system have the answers to the problems that young people are facing?
4. How can the youth deal with the deceptions presented to them in a variety of ways?
5. What can the church do to help the breakdown of family life?
6. Does the church really have an answer?

Those misleading ideas come from the media, the press, the schools, colleges, and the community. Even some churches have become infected with the new viewpoints, values and ideas concerning marriage and the family.

Gender Exchange

Another skew to the breakdown of the traditional family structure is that some husbands, and even wives, are leaving their spouses for the same sex. In some situations, men have left their wives for other men/women, and wives for other women/men. Those behaviours are destroying marriages and family life, thus leaving children even more disturbed. Clearly, if the traditional structure for the institution of marriage becomes defenseless to the changes in society, then this will greatly affect the framework of the family system. Furthermore, if this attack against traditional marriage continues, it will have an aftermath that will be felt for generations to come if we do not wake up and stem the precipitous behaviours that are causing the decline in family life.

The Church

There was a time when the church was the source for compassion and morality. People went there for peace, comfort, solace, in times of trouble, and so on. Pastors were respected with esteem and honour. When parents had a newborn, they took that child to the church to be blessed by the pastor. People felt that being married in a church setting was the ideal thing to do. The community felt safe with the church around. Regrettably, today the church seem irrelevant to those who are godless and immoral in their thinking.

Nevertheless, it is reasonable to say that many so-called Christians and pastors have defiled the name of the God they claim to represent. Their behaviours and style of worship have sullied the title "Christian" and giving it a new definition for greed, faulty doctrines and pride. One of the most unfortunate observations concerning the church is that children are growing up without the knowledge of God, and what He represents in their lives. Seemingly, God is irrelevant to family life and is not included even to take the children to church. If this is the pattern in society then we are gradually sinking into a cylinder of moral decay which will certainly affect both this and ensuing generations.

The School

Similar to the home, the school is where children learn various types of skills as they progress in life. Since school is a more formal setting, the child has the opportunity to learn a wider understanding of socialization, cognitive and emotional development, and government. They learn to make choices for vocational direction and career choices with the help of skillful professionals who will guide them towards their goals.

The school is not only for learning skills, but also to help students become better citizens and to make the right choices. Children learn how to be industrious and to develop character traits which are positive and eventually be productive as they advance in their development. They learn to respect order and authority figures other than their parents with dignity and propriety.

Nevertheless, there are many identifiable weaknesses in the school systems. In some situations, parents have no opportunity to participate in the planning of activities, the quality of education, and the content and choice of the curricula offered to their children.

Another observation is that teachers are seducing students and having sexual encounters with them. These are people, who were highly respected in the community, but some have lost that regard due to the change in morality and teacher-student relationship.

Other Observations include

1. Students are friendly with their teachers whereby they can call each other by first name.
2. There is lack of respect from teacher to student and student to teacher.
3. One can hardly identify who is teacher in some situations because they both dress alike.
4. Teaching has become a "job" rather than a vocation.
5. Parents themselves can be a source of contempt and problems.
6. Students attack teachers who have to defend themselves.
7. Guns seem to be an aspect of the learning tools as children and teachers lose their lives at the hands of classmates and intruders.
8. Bullying has taken a new course where children are choosing to take their lives to escape the intimidation of a bully.

15

Mistakes Parents Make

When we are evaluating children's behaviour, it would be wise to look closely at the structure of family life, the culture, values and principles, and the moral and spiritual ideologies, which they use to govern their attitudes and behaviours. Children learn from the home environment behaviours which they see in their parents.

Admittedly, they also learn from their surroundings, which are part of their natural upbringing. Those learning experiences are of significant values to their moral, social and spiritual development.

The atmospheric backgrounds and life exposures in which children are allowed to be active and creative will be the guiding principles as they develop and grow. This will be their chart for making all kinds of life-fulfillment and life-changing decisions.

Therefore, if the learning experiences are negative and unproductive, the result will be obstruction or destruction to their progress and success in life.

They will certainly make mistakes and behave unseemly, causing pain and disappointment to themselves and problem to those around them.

Frequently, the behaviours are the continuation from previous generations who did not see the need to correct or control negative behaviours in the family line. Instead, violence, moral, emotional and spiritual decadence went unchecked resulting in the next generation being the recipients of past family mistakes. The behaviours set before children should be socially, emotionally, morally and spiritually healthy to enhance their proper development as they face life.

Parents should monitor the types of media entertainment to which the children are exposed from an early age. This can only be done if they take the time to find out the types of programs their children are watching, the friends they keep, books they read and music they enjoy.

In some homes, parents do not care about what happens to their children or what they do because they consider this to be prying into their private lives. In such a setting, it will become an ideal ground for social germs to grow and develop.

Parents must respect their children and teach them the appropriate ways to dress modestly and decently. They should not use foul language to their children or encourage them to lie in any way.

Inherited Family Customs

There are in most families, inherited family customs which descended from one generation to the other through common cultural or social characteristics and behaviours. There seem to be a strong bond when it comes to family rules, beliefs and values whether they are rational or unreasonable.

Despite what outsiders may think; family members bond together by observing their understanding to the meaning of family life and the rearing of children. Similar to the genes and other conditions such as diseases, members of a family inherit traits and beliefs which continue through to successive generations.

It is from those traditions and patterns of behaviour that a mother will train up her children in order to secure the integrity of family customs. For the most part, some of those teachings were faulty causing untold anguish to various ones in the family line.

Sometimes we hear of sicknesses, social situations, poverty, mental and emotional breakdown and other circumstances which we relate to someone in each generation. One of the situations which seem unnoticed is that of childhood abuse.

What makes it generational is that a particular negative form of practice which served in previous generations repeats itself in successive families. For example, in some families women must stay home, and boys follow professional traditions. The first son must have the family name used by previous generations. The methods for discipline remain unchanged even though they do not relate to present culture.

There have been people who will admit that dad, brother or granddad sexually abused the girls, but this was kept a secret. Other forms of abuses included physical in terms of severe corporal punishments. In some situations those events were clear brutality of the child.

For some parents, it was their way of teaching propriety, respectability, and to prevent the child from going astray. Needless to say many of those children grew up hating and even alienating themselves from their parents.

Childhood emotional abuse is an external situation which affects the child internally. For example if the child is insulted or beaten in the presence of others, there is the probability that he will do the same to his children.

If the method used kept the child in obedience and he felt it was good for him to keep him out of trouble, the technique will perpetuate and continues uninterrupted with succeeding generations. In Cindy's family her mother leaned towards the older children, but ignored her by showing open favouritism towards some of the siblings, while she totally rejected her.

Despite her obedience and kindness towards her mother, the response was hostility and lack of concern for her feelings even when the mother embarrassed her.

Counselor and Counselee

Counselor, have you ever tried to talk with your mother to find out why, even at this age being an adult, she is still harsh and hostile against you?

Cindy, I have made several attempts to talk with her but she has always ignored me. She frequently tells me "I am busy," or ignores my call when I try to reach her.

Counselor, when she spoke like that, how did you feel?

Cindy, I was torn, hurt and confused because it is difficult to understand why she does not love me.

Counselor, do you know anything about your mother's background? What kind of life she had as a child...?

The result of the mother's behaviour caused Cindy not to love her own children since she did not know how to love them. Lack of parental love in childhood will continue in the next generation if this custom is not changed. There are parents who do not believe children need love, no matter what the age might. *Everybody needs love*!

16

Parental Responsibilities

Despite how other people live, parents have the God-given responsibility to train up their children in godliness and morality. They should not use the brokenness around them as an excuse for not preparing their children with proper teaching and guidance. Since the home is the first place for learning in the developmental years, parents ought to set appropriate examples before their children which they can imitate. They must keep in mind that their role to nurture, nourish, and love their children should take primary place in their lives and plans. It is not a matter of whether the parent wants to or not; it is godly and morally right to instruct the children with acceptable morals and respect for others.

Another most important factor is that every parent should love the child brought into this world. Since that child did not make the choice to be born, it is the parent's responsibility to show love and appreciation. The child should not feel deprived of love especially in the early years when being loved and appreciated are so crucial to the self-esteem, confidence, and having a healthy emotional life. When love and affection are present, this has a significant impact to the entire being.

Lack of parental love affects a child socially, emotionally and even physically. Whatever happens to any aspect of our lives will eventually have an effect on the physical development especially in a child who is still growing. Furthermore, the experiences during those early years might be the determining factor on how he relates to others and his view of the outside world. This only emphasizes the importance of each parent assuming the responsibility of shaping their children as they develop from birth to when they leave home.

Commitment

When we think of the concept commitment, one can only consider priorities. Not many parents commit themselves to being honest and sincere to their children. There are fathers who will plan a visit, but do not turn up at the appointed time because "something came up," and the choice was disappointing their children. In some of those cases, the child never received an apology.

Commitment means honouring promises and adhering to obligations. The parent who recognizes the importance of responsibility, and duty will do everything to keep promises made to a child. He or she knows the effect failure would have on the child, and would prefer to instead fail someone else. Children are very impressionable and they do not see gray lines. Therefore, when their parents make promises, they expect to see the result of those promises.

Some parents, say they do not know how to relate to a child; their own child. Moreover, by disregarding the child and overlooking his presence in the home is sending out a message to him that the parent does not care about him and will do only the basic necessity when required.

Spending Quality time with them

Spending time with children shows interest in their welfare. Some parents complain that they do not have the time to help with homework because they have to work to put food on the table. In fact, not many parents know their children. Nevertheless, quality time means "quality" with undivided attention and interest.

Making Sacrifices

For some parents, getting a manicure is more important than paying utility bills. They would rather have the gas and lights off, to take care of their own fancies; instead of considering their children's comforts. Therefore, making a sacrifice is completely out of the question when it comes to choosing between the needs of the children, and their desires.

Parents, children are only for a season. While they are young, every parent must attempt to do everything to make that time a pleasant and memorable experience filled with joy and happiness. This does not mean they will always have everything they need, but there should always be love and affection.

Part 2

Life-Changing Events which Affect the Structure of the Family

17

Divorce Hurts Children

One of the most devastating life-changing events which often occur in the lives of children is the divorce of their parents. For some children, the divorce of their parents can be the most painful experience, especially if a choice has to be made between the parents for custody. Children do suffer and some of them carry their feelings into adulthood.

Moreover, when parents' divorce they do not seem to consider their children and the effect of the change on their lives unless it is to the advantage of both or one of them. Seemingly, each parent is planning to meet personal needs and convenience rather than the benefit and support of the child/children.

In some situations, a child may have to travel from one state to the next to spend a little quality time with a parent, and then only to return to the custodial parent. Those types of arrangements give the children an unstable emotional health. This was not God's plan for a healthy family life.

Undoubtedly, the greatest impact divorce has on a child is the decision to choose one parent over the other for residence. Surely, this places a great burden on their young shoulders.

What makes matters worse is when the divorce was a difficult and bitter one and parents squabble in the presence of those impressionable young hearts. Even parents cannot agree with each other, hate one another to the core if they must, but they should not give the children an inkling of bad feelings towards each other.

When parents behave disrespectfully before children, the idea is that they are inconveniences rather than blessings to them. They may not verbalize it, but their very actions communicate those idea.

Here are some examples of the excuses, "I can't keep him because I only have a one bedroom apartment." "I have to go to school at nights and cannot afford a baby-sitter." These are only some of the lava, which spews from the mouths of parents in the presence of their children when a divorce takes place and no one wants to be the custodial parent.

The suggestion is that parents should do their arguing away from their children and not in their presence.

18

Domestic Violence

Another most despicable and emotionally disturbing situation is when a child witnesses the physical abuse of a parent. Fathers will get drunk and return home to physically abuse the mother of their children. A husband will abuse when there is another woman in the relationship and he is trying to get his wife out of the picture. Some do it when the other woman disappoints them and they are despondent and sad. When it is all over the father will try to make up with gifts and flowers to mend hurt emotions and bruised skin.

Apparently, abusers do not acknowledge the dangers of domestic violence and its effect on the entire family. The fact is that the destructive elements of domestic violence affects every member, and spans across relations and generations.

The behaviour contaminates the environment with noxious emotional and social viruses. If any abuser doubts the effect of domestic violence on the children and its implications, the individual only needs to listen to the disappointments of young adults caught up in crimes, gang activities, and illicit sexual behaviours.

Furthermore, when there is evidence of violence in any form, the emotional germs infect everyone with all manner of toxic social outcomes. Obviously, if children spend their formative years in an abusive environment, the experience will affect them tragically, and in all areas of their lives.

Unquestionably, the home should be a sanctuary of love, peace, security, and warmth where children experience tenderness, and a sense of belonging. Therefore, the invasion of domestic violence steals the peaceful contentment all children expect, and in some cases, traps them in all kinds of social and psychological diseases.

Seemingly, it is easier to treat children with drugs to give them peace of mind. However, drugs used in the early years to calm antisocial behaviours, only create a false impression of childhood joys and only make them into robots, controlled by substances.

Domestic violence robs children of the opportunity for normal social development. There can be no excuses for this evil behaviour and furthermore, to have it displayed in their presence is inexcusable.

Those children can become troublesome and disrespectful to those in authority through no fault of their own. Instead, they are hurting, and the only way they can vent their anger is on the outside.

Moreover, the father who abuses his wife in the presence of a child or even in secret is setting the wrong example for the treatment of women before that child. Clearly, if dad abuses mom, that child's life will be miserable, cheerless, and depressing. No child should be the recipient or participant in the violence of a parent.

Regretfully, children all over the world are losing the pleasure of their childhood because parents are not setting the right examples before them. Some children do not know how to behave, handle stress, socialization, interpersonal relations, and other behaviours, which are natural to many others.

Those unfortunate children later become casualties of delinquencies, teenage pregnancies, angry, promiscuities, incarceration, and or early death from drugs or gang activities.

When children witness domestic violence they can display behavioural, social and emotional problems such as depression and low self-esteem. The effect will extend into their school work which might deteriorate as their cognitive abilities decrease due to lack of interest and anxieties.

They may become very argumentative and disrespectful towards parents and teachers. The result of domestic violence in the home can be a long-term situation which continues into adulthood.

19

The Impact of Domestic Violence on Children

I spoke with a grown man, who with sadness in his voice said, "If only I could regain my childhood." I hope parents are listening. Parents, think of what you are doing to your children when you fight in their presence or when you display your hatred and dislike for each other before them. Below are some situations, which affect children who witness domestic violence in the home.

Anger

Children who experience domestic violence are constantly angry. Is it any wonder that a husband will abuse his wife because he is re-living the experience he witnessed in his home, but could do nothing about as a child? Anger is a destructive emotion, but it gets worse when it is covert and has been festering for years. Anger will destroy the best marital relationship, no matter how the spouses love each other.

Emotional Trauma

The presence of domestic abuse and breakup of the family can traumatize children especially when parents are insensitive concerning their welfare. Since trauma is the result of a major event in life, family breakup will make a child become concerned. Children will have to decide which parent to choose, and if they have to relocate. The emotional trauma may result in bed-wetting, stress, low self-esteem, depression, shame, guilt, blame, and embarrassment.

Truly, the traumatic effect of domestic violence will affect the child socially, behaviourally, emotionally/psychologically, physically, and spiritually.

1. *Socially* – it affects interpersonal behaviour. The child can become rude and disrespectful, with loud angry outbursts. The desire for love seems stronger than being sociable and agreeable to gain the respect of others. Their unpleasant behaviour will cause them to lose the friendship of others which they so badly need,

but do not know how to relate their feelings. Instead they display the need in unacceptable offensive attitudes and responses.

2. *Behaviourally* – children will stay away from home to escape either witnessing physical abuses or verbal assaults by a parent.

   Children will also become defensive to a parent even for wrong behaviours. They might be manipulative by making the parent feel guilt for injuring them whether physically or otherwise. For this reason they will make unreasonable demands for what they desire from a parent. Other behaviours include being difficult, acting up, withdrawn, school interruptions or lack of attentiveness

3. *Emotionally/psychologically* – Some children become fearful of losing parents' love or moving from friends when parents' divorce. They will suffer anxiety, embarrassment, and depression mainly when forced to take sides or to lie. There is anger, shame, panic attacks, frustration, confusion, grief, low self-esteem, lack of trust, attention getting, and dependency.

   This dependency can lead to drug-addiction, alcohol indulgence, smoking and inconsiderate sexual encounters. These are evidences of crying out for help, but the parents might be too busy about their own affairs that they do not hear the cry, nor even see the child in the home.

4. *Physically* – Children will complain of headaches and various unspecified sicknesses. Their eating habits might change where they over indulge or they develop conditions which will affect how they deal with over eating.

5. *Spiritually* – There are children who will blame God for the problems in the home believing that He has failed them. They refuse to go to church because according to one person, "I no longer know what to believe."

Domestic violence witnessed by children is a form of provocation because children should be happy in their home where they ought to feel safe and secure.

20

Reaction of Children who *witness* Domestic Violence

1. DV is not only about the two persons involved. Rather it is about the entire family.

2. Children suffer emotional trauma when they witness domestic violence in the home.

3. Children are often asked to choose sides, leaving them more confused and unstable.

4. Children suffer neglect when there is violence in the home because the victim is more concerned about physical safety, security, and protection from the abuser.

5. Children are innocent bystanders who feel hurt, fear of one parent or the abuser, shame, self-blame, confusion, and pain.

6. Sometimes children are the victims of physical abuses.

7. Domestic violence hurts everyone, and when children are involved they can become walking time bombs. They are often forced into adulthood before they are emotionally and financially ready.

8. Children are disappointed when domestic violence is part of their lives because they are optimistic for their parents giving them a happy home life. When hope is lost, they are despondent and confused. They may become depressed and seek out destructive alternatives for comfort.

9. Many children end up being abusers themselves. They will visit it on their spouses or children.

Other situations include the following:

Social Isolation

The child who experiences the physical abuse of a parent has the tendency to be a loner and does not want to bring friends to the home. The disappointment of seeing the separation of parents can also be over-whelming to a child, no matter what the age. Some children are concerned about whether anyone will love them and may not want to form close relationships or even get married because they are fearful. For instance, the girl might decide that she does not want a man to abuse her. Therefore, she avoids marriage or might even turn to her own gender for relationship.

Promiscuity

When there is no love, appreciation, concern, or consideration for the welfare of a child, he/she will go out and seek it in destructive places. Promiscuity will cause the child to become sexually active at an early age, with carelessness and unconcerned about she they goes, or what she does with her body. Everyone needs a sense of belonging. However, if parents are abusive to each other, or fight in the presence of their children, they are tacitly telling them "we cannot give you the love you need, go find it wherever you can." The inference is that the parents are unable to nurture their children with the types of examples and instructions they need to help them, because they too, cannot help themselves.

Seeking Self-Image

There are children who have no more space left on their bodies to place another ring, or etch another tattoo. Those children are crying out for help, for attention. The only way they seem able to gain some form of satisfaction is to mutilate their bodies at the expense of disfiguring themselves, which they will later regret.

Depression

Depression is a condition, which will affects a child who witnessed domestic violence in the home because it upsets the normal routine of life. Sometimes, if a woman is depressed while she is pregnant the effects of her pain will affect the child she is carrying.

In closing, these are only some of the ways domestic violence, affects children. It is a very painful and devastating experience more than parents will ever know, and the consequences are great.

Domestic violence witnessed by a child reaches far deeper than anyone can imagine. Parents should make every effort to keep this destructive beast out of the family, home, and relationship.

Part 3

Parental Emotional Abuse

This section covers the major abuses which a child may encounter during the developmental stages of life. We cannot ignore the fact that every child experienced one or more of these situations.

They include *emotional*, *psychological*, *physical*, *verbal* and *sexual*. These situations will be discussed with vignettes from various individuals and excerpts from interviews.

Names of contributors have been changed, and some insertions will be incidental; yet germane to the type of abuse discussed. What is most important is that childhood abuse of any nature is real and children need help.

The most unfortunate situation is when no one believes the child, and he or she has to bear the pain alone with the lack of support from parents and other significant persons. Those pains are taken into adulthood which may affect every aspect of the individual's life.

Nevertheless, it cannot be denied that childhood abuses are real and must be dealt with immediately. The least a parent should do is to investigate the complaint in order to protect the child from further harm.

There is an old saying that anywhere there is smoke, there is fire. Consequently, if the child reports any form of abuse to a *teacher*, *parent*, *relative* or *family friend* someone should listen.

It does not matter the type of abuse, there should be someone to pay attention, and not ignore that child. When this happens the child is left in danger and becomes vulnerable for the perpetrator to continue with the abuse unnoticed and unabated.

One observation in all situations is that with each person there are similarities and contrasting factors, but they all culminate into abuse of some kind, whether the nature was open *emotional assaults – verbal, psychological*, and *physical* – such as striking or sexual.

A child maybe gripped with silence fearing that someone will not believe him or her. The memory is carried into adulthood which frequently emerges when an event takes place which brings back the incident, causing emotional discomfort.

It is the embarrassment and shame of what took place for which the victims blame themselves, and why some children are silent. In some situations, the child is silent after being told, "It is our little secret."

Child abuse relates to any form of abuses, which cause discomfort, embarrassment, low self-esteem or feelings of inferiority.

21

What is Emotional Abuse?

In its simplest form, emotional abuse occurs when one person *systematically* uses any form of *indignity* [verbal or physical] to *humiliate, manipulate, dominate,* and *control* another person to influence the behaviour of the individual.

As the behaviour continues, the feeling of pain becomes intense and affects the individual mentally, socially, physically, and spiritually. The individual who suffers then begins to build an *emotional structural mechanism of defense* to cope with the constant abuse of the self-esteem, self-worth, and self-confidence.

That coping mechanism maybe over-eating, over-indulgence with substances, and various other forms of comforting situations in order for dealing with the emotional pain being suffered.

Four Stages of Emotional Abuse

Childhood to *Adolescence*: these are most impressionable years when the child looks to parents for love and affection, but these are denied him. Each child responds to emotional and even physical abuses in different ways according to his personality. A child cannot make the right decisions that will help him control his emotions when he is hurting. Parental inconsiderate behaviours which are often negative will cause emotional hurts to the child. If this continues it becomes an aspect of the child's daily life. It is as if he becomes conditioned to expect certain behaviours from the neglectful parent. For the most part, emotional abuse begins in childhood when a child is physically, verbally, or sexually injured. I believe that while someone may overcome some abuses, it is more difficult to bypass verbal abuse.

When a parent tells a child that he/she is unsightly, and uses bitter words to describe and assassinate the child's character this leads to discouragement. Such behaviour sows seeds in the heart of the child, and can be the debilitating factor that will send that child into a negative trend towards a destructive end unless he or she seeks help.

It is during the teenage years when some children begin to rebel against parental abusive treatment towards them. Some may run away, while others might ride it out until they are able to go on their own or go to college.

In some cases, children grow up broken and in despair seeking some kind of comfort to ease the pain of their past. Unfortunately, some may turn to the wrong things or persons for consolation and end up totally broken and without hope.

The teenage years are times of transformation both physically and mentally. This can be a very traumatic experience for the child. There are changes which take place and the child really needs a parent's comfort to help him over those stormy troublesome times. He is trying to find himself and to make decisions about college, career, and relationships.

However, many teens have had to walk this unfamiliar road alone without parental assistance and/or encouragement. If the teen is still at home he may face verbal abuses or witness parental abuse. These are situations which will remain indelible on his mind for which he will seek answers not knowing what to do with the unhappy situations facing him. While he is hurting mom and dad are talking about divorce because they are fighting daily. There are teens who might feel it is easier to end all the troubles destructively and they might go down a path from which they may never return.

The teen age years are critical since the child is making the transition from adolescence and entering adulthood with its many uncertainties and changes. If that child encounters abuses of any kind whether physical and or verbal it will hurt him severely. Although verbal abuse is invisible it will be expressed in behaviour.

The emotionally damaged teenager may suffer from low self-esteem, depression, anger stress and emotional paralysis. Including are feelings of fear and guilt. He might think he is no good especially if he heard this kind of language enough for it to have effect into the psyche – deep into his soul and spirit. It is in adulthood when some of those situations become evident making it difficult for the individual to trust others, and this will affect his relationships.

Young Adulthood: this is the time of transition from the teenage years to adulthood, from 19 years onwards to mid- thirties depending on people's interpretation and conception. The young adult have to deal with the stress of finding answers for childhood hurts and the disappointment he or she feels for being rejected by a parent. If this is coupled with feelings of having a poor body image, this "may lead to eating disorders and then to depression" Craig (1996), p.459.

If the girl is struggling with abuses with a parent this will only compound her already low self-esteem causing her to develop other illnesses and even affect her relationships. What might even make her troubles worse would be if she is a late bloomer and does not have effective signs of maturity while her friends are advancing in physical attractiveness. Nevertheless, if she has a close friend who will encourage her or a mother who loves her, those things will not be so important to cause her to be distressed.

However, the lack of love and affection from a parent will affect her emotional health. If she did not reconcile the hurts of her childhood, this will become a stumbling block in her way preventing her from advancing effectively to the next stage. In fact, if any stage is not completed successfully, it may cause severe problems in the next stage. Still, although a child had been rejected earlier in life, if she gets help later in life or at another stage this can be reversed so that she is able to live a normally with healthy emotions.

Shirley stated that despite the emotional cruelty of her mother all through her life, she has been able to live a normal and happy existence with no emotional complications. This does not say that she does not recall incidences, but she seems more concerned about the state of her mother's mind rather than what she did to her. This is not the same outcome with *Brenda* who is still struggling with the emotional abuses of her childhood. She is hostile towards her parents and refuses to speak to them.

Another person carried the anger of being triangulated by the parents to the point of it becoming her personality. She is always angry, and screams at the least incident. Her husband is unable to console her and sometimes feels helpless stating that he cannot cope with her angry outbursts and wanted to leave the relationship.

Childhood emotional abuses affect each person in different ways in adulthood. Each person responds in his or her own way depending on the severity of the abuse, and whether the individual was able to move on with his or her life successfully.

Middle Age: seems to have some type of enigma concerning its onset and how one realizes that he or she has reached this stage of life. One could conjecture that at this particular stage the individual is at a point in life where decisions have to be made about letting go of the past and reaching to the senior years.

There may be thoughts of disappointments and regrets, loneliness, failures and losses which may come crashing down. These are the situations facing an individual who has to deal with those things because he or she is no longer a child, but rather a grown man or woman and must take responsibility regarding personal concerns. There will be menopause in women and mid-life crises in men.

However, those persons "who take middle age in stride may be fortunate enough to develop a psychological and cognitive capacity akin to wisdom" Craig (1996), p.551. This does not mean that parental rejection goes away or that it is expunge by advanced chronological age. The reason is that this type of rejection was from infancy when the child needed the closeness and support of the parent.

It is at that stage the child learns virtues of trust, love, honesty, and develops self-confidence, self-worth, and self-concept. If the adult is lonely or suffered severe losses and disappointment, these will surface during mid-life when children are gone on their own, and there is no one close to feel some form of comfort. The individual now has the time for introspection and reflection on past activities. She assesses her present state to find out where she can find something to clutch during the times of loneliness.

However, if children abandoned the individual, this might be the straw that will break her sending her into an emotional breakdown with depression and despair. In contrast, if she has well-meaning friends who will support and encourage her, she will overcome the crisis and move on recognizing that these changes are part of life-events which everyone faces.

Since the nurturing of the parent gives the child the feeling of being *wanted*, if the adult who was neglected in childhood faces abandonment whether from children or a spouse this will arouse the old feelings and stimulate the memory of emptiness which maybe she thought she had overcome.

The fact that the adult did not receive that early love from a parent brings about a sense of repetition of the "old order" syndrome. Many hours maybe spent pondering what to do, and that person may even become isolated from friends and family as a choice rather than to face new rejection.

In a conversation with *Clarissa* who is a successful intelligent middle-aged woman, I observed that she was very negative about her lot in life. She insinuated that she felt unwanted and a failure. I was aghast to hear this outburst because I had always admired her as a remarkable woman. She has gone from one profession to another and could well be considered an accomplished person.

Nevertheless, she felt rejected with feelings that no one seemed to care about her. As the conversation proceeded, I discovered that although she acknowledged all her accomplishments there were childhood situations which left her reaching out for love in all the wrong places.

After a failed marriage she has had many affairs which were only short-lived because she was always the only giving and receiving nothing in return. She had an excellent relationship with her children, but her parents were still distant and emotionally out of reach similar to when she was a child. In summing up my understanding of her situation, I realized that she was not emotionally expressive. This was a very sad, yet successful woman.

In this situation, one could assume that while this woman was a successful accomplished person, on the other hand she was extremely disappointed and could not appreciate the advances she made in life. In fact she could not see them because the constant hope for parental love blocked her from facing the reality of her life.

It is clear to see that Clarissa is locked in an emotional paralysis preventing her from seeing her own accomplishments and appreciating what she has. Instead, there is still the need for the fulfillment for parental love.

Situations such as described above will cause regret and insecurity. The reason is that the individual looks back and regrets the inability to win the parents' love, but still has that distance between her and them.

Senior Years: in Erickson's 8th stage of human development *integrity versus despair* which he refers to as "the last stages of life," indicating that, "it is normal for individuals to look back over their lives and judge them. If one looks back over one's life and is satisfied…then one has a sense of integrity. But if one's life seems to have been a series of misdirected energies and lost chances, one has a sense of despair" (Craig 1996, p.60 [8].

In the senior years the individual is facing retirement, loneliness, health problems and various changes in life itself. How she will cope with those events depends on the nature of the event and what is going on in her life. The main fact is that life continues to change, as we grow older.

The physical body changes; children grow older; friends move away; and there may have been loss of job resulting in financial problems. Other problems could be the threat of loneliness and isolation; sickness and fear of death; retirement and many other events that will sometimes bring changes that are hard to deal with. Some of the changes can create fear and a sense of loss, despair and regrets.

Those losses can result in pain that will trigger off former wounds, and this will affect the emotions. It is at such times that the person who has experienced emotional abuse begins to concentrate on life viewing it from the earliest years. All the bad events begin to creep to the surface which may take her on a downward spiral. The rejected person lives with "unrequited grief" because there are no answers to the emotional bombardment she felt throughout life.

The figure below shows the four stages, the progression of childhood emotional abuses, and how each stage interfaces with the other.

Figure 3

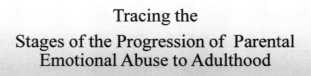

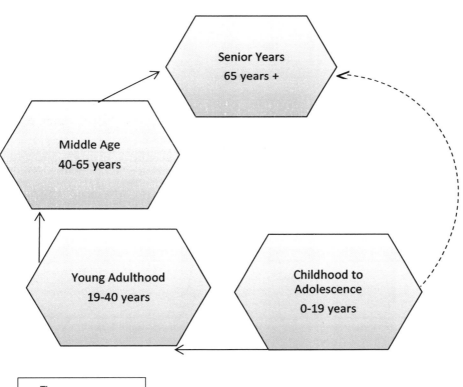

Diagram adapted by B. Stuart, 2014

The age ranges are *estimates only*, since everyone develops and ages differently.

The Origins of Emotional Abuses

It is somewhat impossible to separate and distinguish one abuse from the other since each one impinges on the other.

Physical abuse such as sexual will certainly have emotional consequences as the child considers the painful experience having no one with whom to share the incident.

Some parents blame children for the attack on their innocence and might consider the girl to be the one who entices the brother or step-father.

With some single mothers who are insecure, they might blame the pre-teen for being too precocious and that is why the "boyfriend" touched her or did something wrong.

Emotional wounds are internal and cannot be seen regardless of the nature or origin of the abuse.

With children, the tendency is to ignore the existence of the pain because of embarrassment, humiliation, shame, fear, and an unwillingness to share feelings with others.

Emotional abuses originate from the following

1. *Insensitive and cold Parent/s* – there are parents with unfair expectations from a child who might only be a mediocre student. Yet the parent will nag and discourage him or her to be like another sibling who is on a different level.

   In other situations parents make unnecessary demands, with the use of excessive and harsh punishments on a child. This can be accompanied with physical abuse and other forms of insensitive situations.

2. *Domestic Abuses*: Some children witness physical, emotional, and verbal abuse of a parent.

3. *Spiritual* – legalism, manipulation, control, traditions, rituals. When a spouse demands the other to go to church or to be active in religious activities against his or her will, this is indeed abuse. Each person must be willing to express his or her understanding of God the way he believes until the Holy Spirit intervenes.

4. *National system* – racism; prejudice, unreasonable governmental policies

5. *Economical* – under employed, borderline poverty, national economical unrest

6. *Ourselves* – unrealistic expectations; resentment, grudges, an unforgiving spirit, and holding on to the past.

22

Definition of Emotions

There are four major categories for emotions: *cognitively* through our thoughts; *psychologically*, that is the emotional effect of an event on the individual. For example, if the individual is frustrated, distressed, tensed and so on; *physiologically* through facial expressions, colouring, goose bumps, voice inflections; and overt *behavioural* expressions such as outbursts of anger, distancing, withdrawal and avoidance.

Lazarus & Lazarus, (1994), et al, described emotions as "complex reactions that engage both our minds and our behaviors, thus making them cognitive and behavioral; psychological and physiological".

Emotions can also be described as feelings that evolve from our interpretation of past events that took place in our lives. Those events are cognitively judged and assessed, and depending on the outcome of such evaluations, we then make our decisions as to how we will respond, for example, behaviourally. The choice of response will be based on whether the outcome of the evaluation is negative or positive from our perception.

For instance, if the event seems negligible, it might be ignored as an accidental encounter and not something to harm or hurt. There is an indication here that *value* plays a significant role in making the distinction as to what will be significant in order to decide on a suitable response.

Emotions are further described as life experiences that everyone faces in a variety of situations. The effect of any emotional encounter depends on the force, nature, timing, place and individual who aroused that emotional event. Another important factor is that the emotive person must have some type of interest in the emotion for it to affect the feelings.

After evaluation, the situation must affect the individual in a way to cause emotional pain which will be uncomfortable. The discomfort will motivate action in a manner which will generate some kind of satisfaction. Some people get angry and shout at others or might even turn on innocent ones to overcome the strain of an emotional assault.

However, in order to cope with emotional abuse, many people wear a mask to hide the feelings of abuse. The mask is made up of overwork; substance abuse; immorality and other things.

The reason is that there is shame and embarrassment. Beneath that mask lie fear, sadness, disappointment and many types of emotional and psychological situations, sometimes displayed in hostile behaviours against innocent individuals.

Table 1

Types of Emotional Abuses

Physical	Emotional	Verbal	Spiritual
• Sexual	• Ignoring	• Name calling	• Legalism
• Hitting	• Rejection	• Criticizing	• Doctrine
• Shoving	• Isolation	• Blaming	• Control
• Slapping	• Prejudice	• Threatening	• Manipulation
• Kicking	• Financial	• Use of foul language	• Coercion

Table 2

Symptoms of Emotional Abuse

These are in four categories

Communication	Relationships	Psychological	Spiritual
• Abruptness	• Destructive behaviours	• Obsessive behaviour	• Blaming God
• Manipulative	• Shouting	• Tension	• Lack of interest
• Quarrelsome	• Un-sociable	• Fear, Anxiety	• Resigning from duties
• Brusqueness	• Lack of interaction	• Frustration	• Worldliness
• Aggressive	• Angry outbursts	• Depression	• Complaining
• Argumentative	• Rude	• Feelings of rejection	• Pessimistic about sin
• Difficult			
• Unmanageable			

Adapted by B. Stuart, 2014

23

Emotional Abuse in Childhood

Shirley stated that one of her so-called siblings told her that she is grown and should not be complaining about abuse in her childhood, and it is time to forget and move on. The effect the observation had on her was "demoralizing," reported by her.

Apparently, there are people who consider childhood emotional abuse as incidental and not *that* important as the victim is trying to relate. Despite what others might say or how they might view this situation, it is real with very serious consequences in childhood progressing into adulthood if there was no intervention for healing.

Childhood emotional abuses include, rejection, emotional neglect, ignoring by showing lack of importance, non-inclusion – ostracizing, verbal abuse, putting down – comparing with siblings or other family members, labeling, mocking, favouritism, and distancing.

Many children hide these hurts and become isolated even in school. They refuse to take part in activities and do not make friends easily. They become isolated and may not have a pleasant school experience.

According to *Shirley* she kept to herself and was always alone because there was no one who seemed to have had the time or interest in her pain. Yet, this experience is pain and the effect can be compared to emotional trauma.

The person of abuse may suffer from frightening memories of verbal or physical abuses which hurt so severely that the incident/s leave damaging permanent scars unseen by the human eyes or undetected by a stethoscope.

Each person of emotional abuse will state that it is not the actual abuse, but the emotional impact such as embarrassment and shame which result in pain and distress. It hurts most during childhood when the person inflicting the wounds is someone close, who should show love and appreciation, but in contrast use bitter words and cause pain. No child should be the subject of any kinds of abuses creating stress and emotional discomfort, with feelings of fear and insecurity.

Childhood is one of the most enchanting and magical experiences a child will ever have. Yet, for many the memories proved to be the most *damaging, unfulfilling, unloving, disappointing and painful.*

Therefore, when abuse of any kind is part of the child's collection of memories, it robs him of the wonderful lasting experiences which would cause him to look back with joy when he gets older.

However, when the child is emotionally hurt he or she might internalize the pain from the external situation which caused that hurt. Emotional abuse is invisible and so is the pain unlike physical.

It will not be the nice gifts, lovely home, and expensive vacations that will leave a lasting impression; but the hurtful embarrassing, occurrences of parents' unfairness, emotional outbursts and insults. These are mainly what he takes into adulthood.

Since development is an ongoing situation, if those negative events were not resolved effectively while they are young, the effect will become a recurring nightmare for that individual.

Developmental psychologists noted that between the ages of 12-18 years the child begins to question his identity, beliefs, feelings, and attitudes (Craig 1996). Evidently, it is during this time he is able to distinguish the differences between love and hate, acceptance and rejection.

This stage of the child's life seems very critical, and if negative events are not resolved, there is the probability that they will affect him as he proceeds into adulthood. It is noted that "failure to resolve earlier conflicts often leads to a preoccupation with oneself – with one's own health, psychological needs, comfort, and the life" (Craig 1996, p.60, [7].

This point is confirmed in the situation with *Connie* who stated that since she did not have the love of her father when she was growing she seem to develop a clinging needy attitude towards men and people.

She is always doing things for others even when they did not deserve it. She tries to help in an effort to win the other person's affection to fill the gap left by her father. The problem here is whether the unfulfilled adult is able to navigate around the sense of loss and seeming failure in life in order to find peace and consolation?

For example, if the child did something wrong and he was severely reprimanded whereby the skin was bruised or the emotions fractured, it will not be what he did which comes to mind, but the *severity* of the punishment for his act.

If that was the feedback he received from his offense it will affect his personality and attitude towards authority figures such as teachers and managers.

The impact of emotional abuse in childhood might the cause of marital conflicts and abuses in the family. If someone carries emotional hurt from childhood and did not seek help, the effect of the hurt will be the deciding factor when there are problematic situations causing failures and disappointment.

Anyone who has deep wounds in the soul needs healing and should not hide those feelings of despair and sadness. Still, one cannot help thinking that men are somewhat at a disadvantage when they have been emotionally hurt.

It is possible that they keep that hurt feeling hidden because according to societal reasoning, he is a man and should be able to bear pain. If he were to complain about his feelings he fears being described as being childish, or jeered that he is not a man.

Despite the thoughts others may have about how a man deals with his feelings, childhood hurts should not be minimized because a man who complains about. They do suffer and sometimes deal with the problem in destructive ways such as taking drugs and other form of substances.

24

Negative Images of Childhood Emotional Abuse

"Children can feel rejected because they feel they are a financial burden…have a behavioral problem, born the wrong sex, or are less favored by their parents than a sibling" (Kraft & Morland (1990), p.144. This statement bears out the point that negative emotional incidents of childhood create images which are recalled in adulthood, and sometimes stimulated by a new painful event.

One counselee noted that each time a relationship ended it brought back the memory of when his parent left him. This would drive fear and cause a feeling of great devastation which would take a long time from which to recover.

In another situation the person stated that the mother was inattentive and distant after a painful event.

Counselee: I tried to talk with my mother about an incident at school and was disappointed with her response. She was cold and insensitive and blamed me for the occurrence. Even though I explained that it was not my fault and others were involved. She was very accusative and snappy.

Counselor: How did you feel?

Counselee: I felt empty on the inside and extremely sad and alone. It was as if a hole had been dug inside of me. I could not accept her response. I felt I was left on my own and had no one who cared for me. It was an awfully lonely time.

Counselor: how have you been able to cope with this emptiness?

Counselee: I found myself going into one relationship after another. It was as if I could not help myself because no one cared for me and it was the only way I could find satisfaction to fill the empty place in my heart….

Some children will only remember the bad things they experienced such as a parent's coldness and lack of interest when something bad took place. There are children who reflect on their childhood as being "horrible" because parents were not expressive with affections. Images of childhood which affect relationships in adulthood only prove the effect of parental emotional abuse during those early developmental years.

Childhood is the time when children are supposed to be carefree, happy, impressionable and trusting; they absorb love as the trees absorb carbon dioxide. They love the charms and mystic moments which seem so magical and delightful. They are captivated by the wonders of life and its enigma which makes them inquisitive; and for some, leaves them fearless, invincible as they take risks without thought for consequences.

It may only take one painful event such as parents' divorce for that fearlessness and assurance to shatter into fragments. If followed by abuses from a parent, the child may intentionally resort within himself, unwilling to trust anyone. It is when a distressing event takes place as an adult when some childhood situations which were forgotten return, making the individual take the time to deal with the emotional signal.

Therefore, the initial years are very important concerning what takes place in a child's life since it is during those early years when they are very trusting and vulnerable. They do not dwell on the emotionally damaging unpleasantness received from others, especially their parents. Their aim is to do what is right to earn their love.

Although the child may not ruminate on hurts immediately, yet as he or she develops and similar incidents occur there will be time for thoughtful processing wondering, "Why my mother did that to me?" "What did I do to her to be treated that way?"

Consequently, when a parent hurts a child or disappoints him, it can a have lasting effect even into adulthood. Take for instance a child who was molested by a relative. In some situations when the child reports the incident, the parent often blames her and says, "It was your fault."

Can anyone imagine how this will affect an innocent child? There has to be anguish and emotional pain to think a parent would disbelieve such things especially when proven to be true.

How does one expect a child to accept the rebuke of a parent who has no feelings for his pain, grief, and misery? It leaves the child to grow up with confusion, anxieties, and emptiness.

Figure 2

The Funnel Containing the Negative Images of Childhood

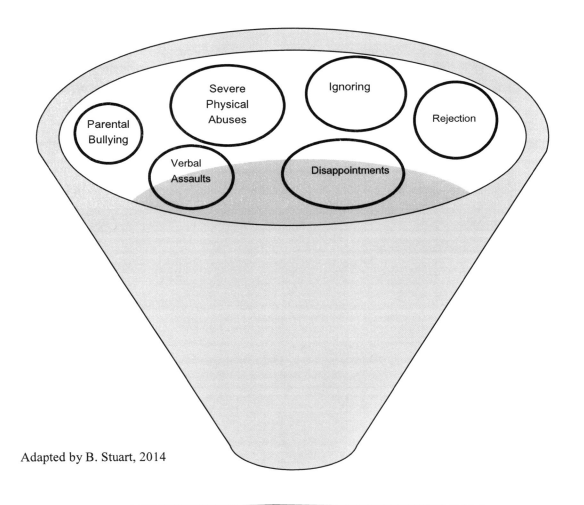

Adapted by B. Stuart, 2014

During the years of development, the child harbours painful situations in his mind similar to the diagram above, unknown to the naked eye, while he or she suffers silently. Each hurtful incident is placed in the funnel, which leaks out in adulthood after another painful situation.

Many families are guilty of this terrible emotional assault on the children of the household. There are times when everyone suffers depending on who is the instigator of the assault.

There are parents who terrorize their children making them fearful with their intimidation and bullying against them.

It does not matter the social background, educational ability or economic strength, emotional abuse will happen in any family setting.

Children post the images of their emotional and physical abuses on the walls of their minds, and these are the memories which affect them when they grow up and face difficulties which they are unable to manage.

In adulthood, challenges in life will cause the hurt individual to become depressed and sad as those negatives episodes return to haunt him.

Images of childhood hurts are just what they are: painful events which took place and which the child could not resolve because of his age and immaturity.

Similar to the circles in the diagram there are differences in nature, strength and sizes and each affects the individual in different ways.

25

Emotional Beehive

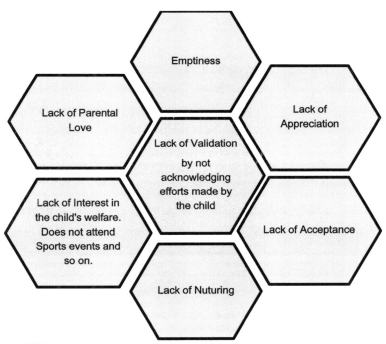

Adapted by B. Stuart 2014

If a child grows up without the essential needs such as love and acceptance required by everyone, this leaves emotional holes. Those holes are unfulfilled necessities which occurred in the life of the child during his development. The situations include lack of love and attention, admiration, warmth, acceptance and validation from parents. These are vital to the emotional well-being of any child, and will pose a great problem in adulthood if he or she did not experience those fundamental requisites when he needed them.

However, if the behaviours demonstrated by parents are negative where there was no love, and lack of acceptance, then the child will grow up with a feeling of inferiority and might think that this the way the world is defined. Therefore he will not expect to be treated any differently by others since the parents did not show appreciation.

Children are so important to life that when Jesus taught His disciples about humility, He *"Called a little child unto him, and set him in the midst of them. And said, Verily I say unto you, Except ye be converted, and become as little children, ye shall not enter into the kingdom of heaven. Whosoever therefore shall humble himself as this little child, the same is greatest in the kingdom of heaven"* [Matthew 18:1-4].

The experience of childhood emotional abuse may begin from the earliest years of infancy when a mother neglects a child, treats him or her with coldness and does nothing to make the child feels a sense of being wanted. This pain may not emerge while a child is young, but when life-changing circumstances face him or her in adulthood, the old pain returns to aggravate and frustrate the individual.

Despite the skillfulness of an individual to hide the horror of the past, there are situations which will uncover and expose those hurts. It is an unconscious attempt to extort some kind of acknowledgement of the emptiness on the inside. The adult feels that somewhere in life he or she lost something which must be found. Is it any wonder why some individuals have only revolving doors relationship? Someone might think that he or she is promiscuous, but entering into the life of the individual one will hear of the painful past and the loss of something such as parental love and admiration.

When disappointments occur in the individual's life, he or she will return to childhood and rehearse moments of humiliation similar to the present event. The old pain returns and there is need for some kind of release; anything which will alleviate or even temporarily reduce the emotional pressures being felt.

While parents may have had their pound of flesh from their children in being harsh and insensitive to their feelings, they do not know the impact their cruelty may have on them when they become adults. No parent wants to know a child is disobedient and or rebellious. However, too many parents have taken a slight remark or attitude from a child to be so serious that their response emotionally and physically, may damage that child for life.

26

Types of Emotional Abuses in Childhood

Some of the evidences of parental childhood emotional abuse experiences include the following situations:

Lack of Parental Love

One counselee stated that, "I was not loved as a child and now I do not know how to love my own children other than to buy them gifts, and scold when they disobey." Clearly, it is the responsibility of parents to inspire their children by loving them. In another situation, the individual said, "I was always seeking for love in all the wrong places. I thought that a boyfriend would fill the vacuum in my heart, but I was mistaken."

Parental love is of vital importance to every child since it is in the home and from parents he or she learns socialism and personality development. Moreover, the child who has a positive interaction with a parent who shows love and teaches respect for others, will be more assertive.

"In contrast, when parents use power-assertive socialization, their children do not develop internalized standards and controls" (Craig, 1996). Using harsh punishment to gain compliance only hurts the child and does not help positively. Therefore, with the use of the right methods to teach, mixed with discipline and sincere love these will work constructively for a child who knows he or she is appreciated.

Undoubtedly, the family has direct influence on the child's comprehensive development (*social*, *cognitive*, *psychological*, *behavioural*, and *emotional*), and any behaviour learned during that period will affect the child all the way to adulthood. Since this is the time when they learn self-esteem and other situations, if there is no parental love that child will grow thinking that if the parents do not show love, there are people who will respond in the same manner. A child will grow thinking there must be something wrong with him or her since the parent does not show love.

Everyone wants to be loved, but when a parent becomes cold, distant, and indifferent he or she makes the environment difficult for the child to penetrate even in times of pain. This unloved situation may take a more acute turn when a parent shows preference to one child or one gender more than the other. All parents have a God-given role to nurture, nourish, and love their children. It is not a matter of whether the parent wants to or not. No child should ever feel deprived of love by a parent. When this happens, it really does something to the entire being.

Lack of parental love affects a child socially, emotionally and even physically. Whatever happens to any aspect of our lives will eventually have an effect on the physical development especially in a child who is still growing. All children need love from their parents, which so many of them deny their children. They do not take the time to show affection and concern for their welfare and day-to-day needs. Seemingly, parents believe it is all right to give up their child to the day care to mind them, while they go off on their happy carefree way.

Favouritism

Favouritism is a negative method used by parents to punish and administer emotional pain to a child whose personality might be different from another. Since some parents saturate themselves in control and abuse of their children, the evidence of favouritism will be easy if it means hurting the one who is not loved. It is painful because it makes the neglected child feels insecure. It is even more painful when the child does everything to gain the love of the parent who might just ignore all those efforts.

Evidently, each mistake seems to be catastrophic and punishment is issued accordingly. The child who is not favoured will find it difficult to accept love or form lasting relationships because of the stressful situation of being unloved by parents.

Unfortunately, the only relationship some parents have with their children, is the freedom to abuse whether physically or emotionally leaving the child depressed, sad and feeling unwanted. Showing favouritism by parents to a child is an emotionally lethal weapon which will injure for life. According to Goldenberg & Goldenberg (1991) "…parents do not respond in the same way to each child in a family, despite their claims to the contrary. Differences in parental behaviour make for significant differences in how each child functions," (p.154).

Candy stated that she lived with a mother and her step daughter. Although *Candy* was the biological daughter, the mother did not show the same affection to her as she did to the step daughter. Moreover, the children of the marriage were of more interest and seemingly more important than *Candy* who was ignored, and does not have the memory of a mother's warmth towards her.

Favouritism hurts and only reveals the distorted mind of the individual who deliberately and willfully gives respect to others for exterior motives rather than for intrinsic values. Moreover in a dysfunctional family all members do not have the same experience and one could relate this to favouritism. In the case of *Candy* the step daughter was of a different culture, whom the mother idolized and praised repeatedly whilst her own child *Candy* was neglected.

The evidence of partiality was considerably difficult for *Candy* who hoped that one day the mother would give her a modicum of love, but this was a futile thought since it never happened. She left home with the constant hope that one day the desire would be realized, but even as an adult, she is still hoping.

In this example, the children of the marriage and the former child of the husband were of more important to the mother, while *Candy* was only a Cinderella to do the hard work in the home. These are some of the childhood experiences some adults deal with, and for some unable to conquer because they believe they have been unfairly treated, which is indeed true.

Closed Environment

A closed environment makes parents unapproachable and unfriendly. In such a setting punishment is often severe, and the gender of the child did not matter. Some of those parents do not allow the children to mix or eligible ones to date. Instead, they are isolated even from relatives and only attend functions when the parents chaperone.

In some homes, children are not encouraged to express themselves. Some husbands deny their wives self-expression, and the home seems to be constantly under mental siege. One can only assume that from those homes you might find children who are lonely, moody, irritable, frustrated and with all kinds of emotional disorders.

Unfortunately, some of those children bring those behaviours into adulthood especially if they had no treatment in their youth. A closed system is dangerous for children who live in such an environment. One could further infer that those children will eventually revert to substance abuse to fill the emptiness in their lives.

Emotional Neglect

Neglect comes in many forms, but the method of administration is *ignoring* the child by not demonstrating interest in him or her except if is "absolutely necessary" (Sarason & Sarason (1996, p.438). The parent will provide basic needs such as food, educational, health or shelter, but deny the child of emotional encouragement or support. Those parents are often involved in other things such as careers or activities which stimulate their interest. They leave their children to caretakers who might only offer professional interests, but not parental love.

Sarason & Sarason further noted that, "Neglected children show the effects of lack of parental stimulation. They talk less and make fewer social responses," (p.438). There are situations when parents consciously or unconsciously repeated the style of parenting they observed from their parents with their children.

Some parents are inattentive to the emotional needs of their children. This lack of sensitivity can be passed down to generations. Another form of emotional neglect could also be fighting and arguing in the presence of the child, not caring how he or she feels about the disturbance.

Emotional Abandonment

In childhood emotional abandonment could be when a parent, for example a dad, is often absent maybe for work or he is an itinerant parent. The feelings of rejection may emerge when the absence becomes extended. This makes the child stop expecting to see him and might resort to the inner self as relinquishment of ties continues to disappear.

The feelings of rejection might make the child become very angry from the teenage years, and in the case of a girl she might develop fear and anxiety when it comes to trusting men. It would be easy to harbour negative feelings against men that they ought not to be trusted because of dad's failure. Eventually, either she will choose the wrong person who might be an abuser or mistreats someone who would care for her.

Emotional abandonment is critical because it does not only affect the child in the early years, but continues into adulthood and may even affect the relationship with God. The spiritual effect could be when God seems to take too long to respond to prayers and requests. The now adult, compares God with the neglectful parent, and will begin to resent Him, and finds it difficult to accept His love or trust Him.

Shirley stated that her mother's treatment towards her caused her to think that God did not love her, and His treatment was no better. It took her many years to understand that God loved her and should not be compared with her mother's behaviour. There were times when she prayed about something which she did not receive at all or at the time she required it.

During the time of waiting or what she thought was a "no" she would then consider God's delay an act of punishment similar to what the mother would have done. She referred to a time she wanted to see a movie with the other children. That evening the mother gave money to everyone, but deliberately refused her in the presence of the others. As a child in the home, she felt abandonment from the mother and she herself, kept apart to avoid insults and physical abuses.

Despite the fact that one may think that abandonment is only physical, it is not. Emotional abandonment becomes evident when there is no nurturing, warmth, love, companionship, spontaneous communication exchange, and adultery. In the case of adultery, it is evident that the offender no longer desires to have close relationship with the other spouse, and therefore turns to others' for fulfillment.

Parental Rejection

Rejection is not a situation that many people are capable of dealing with at any time of life. The reason is that rejection is a negative emotion which leaves scars throughout the life of the individual, and in some situations, the memory will affect the marital relationship.

Parental rejection lasts longer than most other situations which a child will encounter because of the refusal to acknowledge that child as a person who needs love, nurture, and attention. It gets even worse when that child is made to feel inferior to other siblings. Usually the rejection begins from conception if the mother did not plan for the child and does not want to abort. It cannot be denied that one of the greatest memories a child will have is the love of a mother and when this is missing it is discouraging for the child.

Despite his feelings, if the situation is not dealt with or resolved early in life, the individual may take the rejection into other relationships, or his own family and the cycle begins all over again. This is where faulty inherited family behaviours exist and dominates parenting.

Furthermore, if that relationship turns out to be an unfaithful marital situation, this will ignite the past hurts of rejection and make the woman feel disappointed with herself or even with life. It is very difficult for someone who has faced parental rejection to deal with marital rejection successfully without professional intervention, and the help of God's Holy Spirit.

Besides, "The most painful kinds of rejection occur during the earliest years of life – preschool and the early grades – because there is no way of explaining the reason for an action which infants or children interpret as rejection" Seamands (1993), p.299. Children cannot reason as do adults and depending on their age, will not understand the humiliation of a parent or her rejection.

Nevertheless, when a child is rejected by a mother, this is more painful than a father's, because of the symbiotic attachment from the womb. No one should criticize a child/adult who still hungers for a mother's love. This love is unique and special; when denied it leaves a hole in the heart of the individual which only God can shut.

Age means nothing to the need for a mother's love. There is no statute of limitations to close that door; it is always open to receive that love. If the mother has died, the child might find a substitute, but it is when the mother is alive and continues with her rejection. It is one of the most painful experiences any human could ever know.

Indeed, parental rejection is one of the worst situations a child will suffer. While a father might be separated from his child who might get over the absence, with the neglectful mother the effect lasts a lifetime. The reason is due to the symbiotic bond between the mother and child during those nine months of gestation.

Those months are important to both because there is a *natural interdependent binding* relationship with the two. Therefore, if the mother leaves that child in the early weeks/months or years, the separation might be critical to the child's entire development, especially the emotional aspect of his or her life.

Nevertheless, many mothers seem unconcerned about their relationship to the newborn, and how critical expressions of love and warmth are in those early experiences. If the mother ignores her newborn and this continues where there is no caring shown, that child will grow with an emptiness of unfulfilled love. There are situations where emotional hurts affect the child all the way to adulthood.

Listen to the individuals below:

---*"My mother gave me up when I was baby. I have always sought for love and usually in all the wrong places because there has always been that emptiness inside of me. I am an adult now with children and grandchildren, but the hurts and emptiness still exist within me.*

---*"I discovered that mine left me when I was a toddler. They told me that I regressed to infancy, and this has affected my physical growth and development. Throughout my life I have been searching for ways to get my mother to accept and love me, but to no avail."*

---*"My mother never showed loved towards me. I felt her rebukes, physical and emotional hurts. It did not matter what I did for her or what I gave her, she would not budge. Instead, she loved her other children born from her marriage.*

I have always admired my mother, but she would only shout at me and put me down. When one of my sisters spoke harshly to me with insults, my mother only laughed at me."

---*"I do not know what it is to be loved by a mother. I cannot remember a time when she put her hands on me, except to hurt me physically. Sometimes, I think she hated having me, but did not say so other than to abuse me emotionally and physically.*

---*"My aim was to do anything to please my mother with the hope that she would one day say, "I Love you," but it has never happened. I no longer need her in my life.*

I am over her now and I do not cry when I think of her abuses, lack of love and neglect to me as a child. She still has not shown appreciation or concern for me.

---*"Although for many years she often comes in town to visit her children, yet she has never called me or shown interest to be with me. I used to cry and cry for hours during my childhood.*

In my tears I would say, "Nobody loves me while she and her husband would jeer. It did not matter to me, I just kept on crying."

---*"My mother refused to admit to the pain she caused me as a child. Even before she died I tried to reason with her, but she was adamant against me and did not reconcile.*

I am still hurting even though I have my own children to love me. There is emptiness and longing in my heart for the love of a mother."

Humiliation

Parental humiliation is a direct attack on a child's emotions. It cuts deeply and pierces the very innermost of the being. When added to other incidences this will only crush the child making him or her become withdrawn and even physically ill with headaches, stomach aches and psychosomatic symptoms. Psychosomatic symptoms are physical feelings of psychological situations. Parents humiliate children with criticisms, and the use of harsh insulting words.

The Bible teaches "Children, obey *your* parents in all things: for this is well pleasing unto the Lord" [Colossians 3:20]. With this admonition, parents do insist upon obedience from their children in all things. However, how can one expect a child to be totally obedient when a parent humiliates and embarrasses him or her in the presence of others?

Parents who do such things are insensitive and cruel. While they may expect the child to be obedient, it does not stop there because for the obedience to be completed there are scriptural guidelines for parents.

In the same passage we read, "Fathers, provoke not your children *to anger*, lest they be discouraged" [Colossians 3:21], which abusive parents often ignore when they are issuing insults, labeling, and name-calling to the child. Personally, I believe the onus is on the parents because if they set the example, the children will follow.

Social Isolation

The child who experiences abuse might believe that he is bad and that is why mom or dad abuses him. The girl might think she is not pretty like mom or another child and this is the reason why she is not loved, and is the recipient of abuse. According to Craig (1996) "social isolation is a common characteristic of families troubled by child abuse" p.379. Social isolation has another skew whereby parents keep the children from having friends and from relatives.

Part 4

The Effect of Childhood Emotional Abuse in Adulthood

The effect of childhood emotional abuse begins from the womb, to the unfulfilled desires of the child to be loved by a parent. The absence of parental love might make the child become withdrawn stressed, and insecure. Childhood abuse affects the entire development of the child: *cognitively*, *emotionally*, *socially*, and *psychologically* extending into adulthood.

In one situation *Mary* who did not have the love of her mother who rejected her at an early age, described her sexual behaviours resulting from seeking love in all the wrong places. This also includes choosing wrong alliances and staying in an abusive relationship which threatened her life. The reason why she stayed in the destructive environment, she felt that if she left there would be no one to love her. This misconception is common among adults who were emotionally abused as children, and did not receive treatment for their pain.

The child who has experienced and suffered emotional abuses feels its consequences very deeply. The pain has a great impact and will prolong into adulthood. For many children, when they grow up there is difficulty in responding to love and appreciation because they do not trust those who try to show affection. It is difficult to open up to anyone fearing there will be disappointment.

Seemingly, those children are still living in the past, which becomes a hindrance so that there is difficulty in accepting love, unless they are able to give something in return. Those hurt children conceptualization of love becomes a quid pro quo generalization of human relationships either for positive or negative results.

Since their parents reprimanded them for mistakes but loved other siblings because of natural abilities, gender, or attractiveness; this is the way the world behaves. This is understandable since in many homes children have to prove themselves to receive attention or a parent's love.

In a situation where there was an incident of breach, the parent may not express love, but instead meet the misdemeanour with physical or verbal abuses.

Children who suffered any form of abuses are left confused because their perception of parents is to receive love, warmth, and sincere consideration. When these are missing they cannot comprehend the reasons because they are confused and unable to grasp any understanding for a parent's rejection or harsh words.

Emotional abuses are not visible as those which are physical. However, children can and may show signs by their behaviour. Those behaviours might only be noticeable to the trained eye; otherwise they might be dismissed and mistaken for rudeness or other underlying causes.

Although we cannot assign all emotional disorders to childhood abuses, there are situations which stand out clearly, such as spousal or to one's own children could be the direct result of childhood emotional hurts.

In this section, various kinds of effects relating to childhood emotional abuses will be discussed. These were chosen since they are what have been disclosed, and shown to be correlating to parental abuses to their children.

27

Relationship Problems

Emotional Prostitution [EP]

Emotional prostitution occurs when the individual uses the body as currency for a man's love even when that man is abusive. While others will sell this commodity for monetary gain, the emotionally hurt individual uses sex to gain approval from a man.

Sometimes we wonder why any woman or man would remain in an emotionally and physically toxic relationship. All evidences show that there is danger and constant abuse; but when one explores deeply there is low self-esteem and neediness which keeps the victim trapped in a distressful and sometimes dangerous relationship.

In closer encounter the individual will admit that the relationship is uncomfortable, but there is a need for companionship. A child who was starved of love and attention will seek approval from others in adulthood, sometimes in all the wrong places. They do this in many ways and EP is one of those situations.

Inability to have healthy relationships with the opposite sex

When a child has been emotionally starved during the early years, he or she might become very angry with the self and even accept blame for being born as the reason for a parent's neglect. This faulty belief and low self-concept could be the reason why some women give themselves easily with the hope they will be loved by the men in their lives.

Some children blame parents for not being present or not teaching them about relationships. There are women who will admit that they do not know how to relate to men in a meaningful healthy way other than to have sex.

They compare all men to be the same only to have sex and then leave. In most of those situations the woman feels that sex will cause the man to remain and love her. She disappointingly discovers that he only needed her body, and not her.

The woman with the need for love and acceptance will accept all the nice words which make her feel wanted. She will trust the most abusive man if he shows any kind of interest in her.

It does not matter how he treats her even when she complains, there is the tendency to remain with him despite the number of times they separate. There seem to be no inner strength to leave a sick relationship because she keeps going back because of the blindness to the injustices, abuses, selfishness and lack of real love.

Women who find it difficult to relate to men in a positive way are only able to reach them in a codependency manner. They mistakenly believe that by pleasing a man at their expense he will in return give sincere love. Those women are needy and empty on the inside despite their evident successes and accomplishments in life.

Some women can only relate in a romantic manner, but outside of sex they feel insecure and uncomfortable. Seemingly, every man is a replica of dad who was harsh, cold, and unfeeling.

Lack of Trust in Relationships

In some situations, the individual might be resentful of someone he or she thinks who is trying to be a mother. A husband might tell his wife that she is not his mother regardless of what she does for him. There is lack of trust and constant emotional outbursts. It is difficult for the individual to form lasting relationships and this could be the result of fear and insecurity. The rationale is that if my mother did not love me, no one else does.

Emotional Inconsistencies

Cognitive Dissonance

Festinger 1963 describes cognitive dissonance as "the non-fitting relations among cognitions," also that "it is a motivating factor in its own right." It is the incongruent relationship among cognitions of thought and understanding which often causes stress. Therefore, the abused child seeks understanding concerning the parent who says, "I love you" yet, turns around and hurts her. The behaviour is inconsistent and contradictory in relation to what is said, and that which she experiences from the parent.

Shirley reported that her mother told relatives that she loved her, which of course, she did not believe. Even when she tried to explain to relatives the abuses of her childhood and the experiences of neglect, the mother would adamantly say, "I don't know about that." She has always denied and never admitted to her fault. Moreover, she stated that she picked up the phone one day to ask her mother's forgiveness because she felt led to do this. However, when she thought the mother would have at least said, "I am sorry if I have ever hurt you," it never came.

Counselor: how did you feel?

Shirley: to this day, I am still appalled. She must have felt that she had a right to mistreat me, and there was no need to say "sorry."

Counselor: what did you want to hear from your mother?

Shirley: only to say, "I am sorry I ever hurt you."

Counselor: how do you feel now?

Shirley: I am truly sorry for my mother.

Counselor: what will you do now?

Shirley: I will continue to keep my distance because she has not shown interest in me. Even though I have sent gifts to her, she does not acknowledge them. My concern is how can she say to anyone that she has nothing to be sorry about, while all through my life I have complained about her cruelty to me? I am saddened because I am wondering where she is in her mind or if she is just being dishonest.

Counselor: why are you sad? Why should this matter to you?

Shirley: I am sad because she says one thing and does another. It makes me wonder if I am sure of the things I remember which she did to me...

Clearly, cognitive dissonance leads to intra-psychic conflict which is one of the psychological problems that the child will encounter from parental abuse. There will be a constant struggle with trying to find answers from the inconsistency of the parent's behaviour which could not be understood during childhood. However, as the child grows older and is able to comprehend she will critically re-assess the behaviours to conclude that the parent was not being fair or true.

Based on this awareness, she will judge the intentions of others. It will be the outcome of the evaluation which will motivate her to make decisions concerning relationships; whether they are rational or reasonable will be insignificant.

Other psychological consequences in adulthood related to childhood abuses could be the result of unresolved situations held over from childhood (See Sarason & Sarason, 1996; Eaker-Weil & Winter, 1993; Brown, 1991).

In some situations, the result of cognitive dissonance will show itself in the behaviour of a woman who knows that a relationship is destructive, yet she cannot pull herself away because of the need for love.

For example, despite the discomfort she experiences from an abusive boyfriend she will remain with him because there are times when he shows love and attention which she needs.

It is those moments of relief which gives her a sense of being "loved." She finds it very difficult to give up this person because he often fills some need in her life. Others will indulge in substances even though they know they are unhealthy.

The evidence of cognitive dissonance in a painful relationship, occurs when the woman has to make a choice whether to leave or remain regardless of the dangers. For some women, it is as dangerous to remain and might be even be worse after leaving. This is where the struggle begins and intra-psychic conflicts becomes even more intense.

Negative Dissonance

In a situation where a woman is able to experience some love from a harmful relationship, over time she might decide that it is not going anywhere and will break away. If she has the courage to leave, in retrospection she will blame herself for allowing the relationship to have gone the length of time it did. She realizes that she made a mistake and should have walked away but could not.

According to (Vander Zanden, 1988) "negative dissonance exists when the individual makes the wrong decisions about a conflicting life event.

It will be the wrong decision which the woman made that will aggravate and frustrate her, and not so much the abuses.

She will blame herself forgetting that the boyfriend had a part to play in her unhappiness. Until she is able to confront herself realistically, noting that everyone makes mistakes, she will continue to beat upon herself or seek professional help for the problem.

28

Psychological Effects

With psychological problems, these often manifest themselves in high-risk behaviours. Those problems become evident when the child gets depressed, anxious and withdrawn. Unfortunately, some parents do not always pay attention to changes in the life of the child, either because they are too busy or they just do not care. Sometimes there are multiple fathers, and the hurting child might be from a previous relationship.

Shirley reported that her father lived in another state, and she was the only child for him whom the mother had before marriage. When she was about seven years of age, the mother married someone else and had multiple children for the husband. Although the mother left her with relatives at an early age, from the birth of the first child she saw the change in the mother's behaviour.

In fact, she stated that the mother became cold and indifferent which got worse until she had to leave home in an attempt to escape the neglect, insensitivity and lack of love. For her, there were times when she thought of running away from home, but was too scared that something terrible might happen to her. According to her, in those days she was always very fearful and wondered how she would have managed when she grew up.

Shirley recalled days of fear, loneliness and depression since she had no one to talk with. Her depression would be with crying day after day while the mother and her husband would mock her. The husband made comments to the effect that she would not amount to anything worthwhile.

This made her cry even more because the mother said nothing. She said the mother was brutal and unmerciful. Although she has grown and showed kindness to the mother, she has not reconciled or acknowledged her as a daughter.

I remember when she came to see me still crying, broken and distraught wondering why her own mother could reject her all the years of her life. She asked, *"What could have broken in my mother's heart that she cannot love me the way she loves and cares for her other children?"*

It was difficult to be distant as a counselor, and to be objective with such a case as Shirley's. Still, as all therapists will report, there is always one which stands out the most, when it is impossible not to be human. The aim of counseling must always be to help the hurting in order to restore a measure of confidence, hope and security for a better life and future.

The psychological effect of childhood abuse can be long-term if the individual had no recourse.

For *Shirley,* although she often complained to her father he could not help her because he had another family and moreover he lived thousands of miles away. She was virtually at the hands of her emotionally and physically cruel mother. She was humiliated, laughed at and intimidated by the first child of the marriage, while the mother looked on, listened and often laughed at the demeaning way the other child spoke to *Shirley*.

Psychological emotional abuse in childhood is indeed lasting and needs special treatment with great concern for the hurting because the effect of it will take many paths, and affecting many channels in the child's life. Its effect in adulthood is evidenced in the following situations.

A

Low Self-Esteem

The emotionally impaired adult will seek identity through the people he or she interacts. There is a constant need to belong, but how to, presents a problem since there is always the desire to please. The individual has no confidence or even self-respect despite how successful that person might be.

Shirley said her self-confidence was shattered at about the age of eleven years when her mother looked at her and said, "*Sin is what made you ugly because you were not born this way.*" She said that for years she wore the label of being "ugly" and would not laugh for anyone to see her face. Instead, she would always hide or hold her head down so no one saw her.

The change came after she had her second child, when someone at her workplace remarked "*you are always looking attractive: no matter what you wear.*" That day her change came and she was delivered from her fear of others seeing her laugh. She was no longer uncomfortable and ashamed of who she was or what she looked like.

Another thing which help Shirley over-came her mother's meanness was looking into the mirror often and saying, "*you are one beautiful woman: world, here I come.*" This always helped her get over the memory of the past and the label her mother placed on her. Low self-esteem is a destructive tool placed in the hands of cruel people when they use hurtful words against another human being.

Janice stated, "I have lost my identity and no longer know myself." After a lengthy painful relationship the time came to break off, but how to cope and move on for this person was a great problem. For her, the lost "friend" was able to meet certain romantic needs, but nothing lasting. The emotional needs were unmet because no person can meet those needs without the help of the hurting.

Sometimes the persons we expect to meet our emotional needs were recipients of childhood abuses themselves, and are seeking the same love and affection as the one who is hurting. The difference is that each person deals with hurt differently. One individual will hide it under a smile, drink or such like while another acts out in some way or another.

The person with low self-esteem can become trapped in gloom and despair unable to face life-changing circumstances. This prison can spiritually and emotionally paralyze the individual who will resort to substances such as drugs, smoke, and alcohol as remedies or comforters for the pain. Seamands (1981) noted that, "Satan's greatest psychological weapon is a gut-level feeling of inferiority, inadequacy, and low self-worth" [p.42].

With *Janice*, being alone was the worst thing that could happen in her life. For this reason it was from one relationship to the next seeking for love in all the wrong places.

Childhood emotional abuse will make the individual think of himself as being inferior and not deserving even the love of God. Each time that person does wrong; there is the feeling of being judged with the expectation of accompanying punishment similar to what a parents' response would have been.

B

Fearfulness

One of the reasons for fear is the thought of displeasing the object of emotional pain. Even though a parent may be harsh and insensitive, this does not prevent a child from still hoping for that day of reconciliation when the parent will show evidence of appreciation. For this reason the child will make every effort to please rather than cause distress to the parent.

Shirley stated that although her mother was cold and distant towards her, though not to the other children, she feared her and would not show pain even when she was ill. This was her way of trying to please the mother. She would also absent herself from school for some frivolous reason to stay at home and help with the hope that the mother would acknowledge the sacrifice, but it did not work. Nothing she did motivated her mother to love her. At times the mother seemed to have been ashamed of her looks and would not speak well of her when other people were around.

When asked why she feared her mother her response was, "*She always shouted at me. There were times when she laughed and mocked me, but I still loved her because I had hoped that one day she would say, "I love you."*

I was afraid to express myself because I felt that by holding back this would cause her to be kind to me. It did not work."

With *Chandra*, she feared her dad's discipline since he was so harsh and unfeeling. He struck without mercy and compassion not caring that this was a girl. She wondered if in his mind he was thrashing her as though someone else to whom he owed some revenge.

C

Change in Personality

Life-changing events which cause pain can also change our personality because any painful event will and may change our temperament and behaviour. For example, someone who was happy and trusting may turn into someone fearful and difficult in relationship. That person may become fixated on a past event questioning why it happened, and how she could have prevented the occurrence.

When changes occur there are many perspectives from which we seek understanding concerning *what* and *why* the event took place. Sometimes we understand, but there are times when we cannot find any reason or cause for our circumstances. Since changes come from many sources we are able to eliminate some things.

Someone said, "*I no longer laugh, and it seems as if I do not know myself anymore.*" This person complained of anxiety, fear, and emotional pain, stating that each day she was losing a part of herself and no longer knew who she was; it is as if she had no identity

Personality change as a result of emotional abuse can be evident in behaviour from thought pattern or cognitive domain. If the individual believes that he or she has been unfairly treated, this thought will be the fundamental base for behavioural responses. It is not so much a catharsis effect, but the end product of cognitive evaluation from the premise of what is fair and what is not.

The cognitive-behavioural response may not take place until when the individual reaches an age to reflect, assess, and compare what is normal parental love to that which is abnormal. As an infant, his only concern is to be loved and he was unable to fully understand the differences between implied or actual abuse. This will be veiled especially if the parent shows some type of tangible thoughtfulness such as giving a birthday gift.

Personality change resulting from emotional abuse is real and not a fiction of one's imagination. However, whether we are directly involved or outside factors are contributors to hurts, the fact remains that we hurt. The hurt person tries to make sense of events with questions for which sometimes there are no answers.

Emotional events affect us spiritually, psychologically, and physically. Some of those events which take place include family dysfunction, gender crises, career choice, marital and various kinds of relationship situation.

Despite the disappointments in life, a positive person, who has faith, will adjust his or her behaviour to cope with changes in order to find balance, and to prevent being overwhelmed with failure or setbacks.

Unfortunately, some people do not accept failure and disappointment as do others. For some, a small set back might be devastating and difficult to face. Those persons either move too far to the left or right depending on their worldview and interpretation of the event. Those who are hard on themselves give up easily, and will allow emotional hurt to hold them in bondage all through life.

A decision which turns out to be a disappointment might cause an individual to think he or she is no good. Therefore, the cognitive understanding about an event plays a major role in how an event will affect an individual.

D

Emotional Dependency

Emotional dependency means that the individual relies on others' to fill emotional needs rather than from inner strength. There are doubts about personal abilities; therefore the individual may only draw strength from those who will give encouragement. Those persons do not accept failure and disappointment as normal life situations. When those circumstances occur this can be overwhelming to those persons who depend on others to support them and hold them up when they are weak.

One theory given for dependent individuals is that they "had overprotective parents who made life so easy for them as children that they never learned coping skills" Sarason and Sarason (1996), p.259. This is where I differ when referring to *a counselee.*

According to this individual, although the parents were overprotective to all the children, it was not to make life easy for them. Instead, it was to keep them away from outsiders even their own relatives. They were extremely severe and demanding, which made life very unhappy and difficult even for self-expression. Even as an adult, the individual finds it very difficult to cope with the least life-changing situation.

Sarason and Sarason (1996) further stated that "Dependent individuals try to make themselves so pleasing that no one could possibly wish to abandon them…they feel they must act meek and obedient in order to hold onto other people (p.258). This point bears out strongly with *Jaida* who was very shy, kind and conciliating but seemed unable to care for herself though a grown person.

Seemingly, there was a constant need to have a man around who would give compliments which would soothe her, even though many times the individual proved to be insincere. Yet, *Jaida* would go out of her way to do things to please the person in her life with the hope that the relationship would last.

E

Emotional Paralysis

If a child suffered an extremely painful event which shook him to the core of his being, this one experience can have an adverse effect to leave him in a state of emotional paralysis if he was unable to express himself or if he did not receive adequate help even the compassion of a parent. There are parents who are icy cold and insensitive towards a hurting child. They would rather blame the child for an incident instead of showing love and thoughtfulness, helpfulness and being kind.

In the case of a parent and child, this might the result of what came down through the generations to stand firm even when there are reasons for expressing sympathy about an incident. It would not be too extreme for considering faulty generational beliefs to be a sign of emotional paralysis, which will hinder the progress of family members even though they cannot see anything wrong with their methods for dealing with difficult situations.

How could any parent display hardness toward a child who is hurting? Evidently, the child will be disappointed with the way the family handles problems. However, if former members of the family were comfortable with the technique used for problem solving, whether it was substantial or not, others will follow.

The reason why faulty generational approaches to family problems continue through successive ones could be that members of the existing generation are unable to extricate themselves from the teachings of the past. In order to correct the error, new members must attempt to educate themselves with behaviours which will take them out of the quagmire of defective teachings, and unsatisfactory cultural customs and values and end the hurt to their children.

Sometimes, parents hurt their children but do not know that what they are doing is wrong because that was the way they were brought up. However, parents who wilfully physically hurt their children and then say, "Shut up, I will give you something to cry about," will cause that child to learn to hold back hurts and not express pain no matter how excruciating. The threats of the parent will paralyze the child with fear who might even wet his pants just hearing dad approaching. He knows that if he continues to cry from his pains, there will be more abuses, so he keeps quiet and immediately shuts off his emotions.

Shirley feared her mother. During a childhood illness the mother took her to the doctor. However, when she left her at home with a caretaker, *Shirley* cried from her pain and discomfort brought on by the illness, but as soon as the mother appeared all the crying dried up. The mother was very cruel and abusive. The fear dried up her pain until the mother left.

Here we see that the mother's abuse became a deterrent to the child so that even when she was in pain there was restraint to avoid being bullied or physically abused. This child was not able to express the fear, but instead internalized it. From her description of her childhood, she was the only one who was unable to express her emotions. She was always anxious and all through her childhood there was a sense of fear about the minutest thing.

A parent might tell a boy if you cry you are a sissy. For the girl she will be a cry baby. Therefore to avoid being labeled or insulted, the child will quickly act bravely and please the desires of the parent. Could this be the reason why there are people who hurt others with no remorse? Maybe a husband will say he loves his wife, yet he beats her at will and with no provocation from her. It is as if those who are emotionally paralyzed do not care about the feelings of others since they do not express their own.

Maybe one could associate emotional paralysis to conditioning. If a behaviour which causes a child to restrain his emotions is repeated enough times, eventually it becomes automatic and he does not have to think about performing it. However, when an event occurs to stimulate the required behaviour of restraint, it will happen unconsciously. He does not have to exert any effort to carry out the procedure of being insensitive to things which should cause him to respond with interest and empathy.

It would not be extreme to say that police men, doctors, counselors, and clergymen, have learned behaviours which make them emotionally paralyzed when they give disappointing news to a family.

Although psychologists state that, "children learn, from a very early age, that open displays of negative feelings are unacceptable in public places…" (Craig 1996, p.300), should children restrain the way they feel about pain, abuse, and insults? Should they not be able to express themselves even in a controlled manner? Nonetheless, while they may want to do so, fear, cultural beliefs and family backgrounds such as generational faulty values may hinder them.

While a child must learn to manage emotions such as anger, nothing is wrong with being angry if something irritates him or her. No child should live in such fear of his parents that he cannot express himself to say what he likes or what he does not like.

For example, if a child has an aversion to eating certain foods, not that they are bad for him, why must he be forced to eat them to please mom or dad? A situation such as this will cause a child to shut off his disgust for the particular food, and eats it only to please the parent.

The reality of emotional paralysis is that the individual shuts off his feelings and is unable to feel emotions as do others. In order to help this person he has to unlearn the negative way of responding to pain, and accept the fact that we all have emotions which are necessary to life.

Furthermore, a child must learn that nothing is wrong with expressing emotions if the action is with care and consideration for others.

Similar to how he can be in control of not expressing his emotions, he can also allow them to emerge and control them in an acceptable manner. So long as the individual is aware of where he is, what is acceptable and what is not, he should be able to express himself in an orderly manner so that he can be comfortable and happy.

F

Emotional Pain

When an incident occurs in an individual's life over which he or she has no power, the inability to find a solution for relief will cause that disappointment to lodge in his mind, causing emotional pain. The more he thinks about the incident the angrier he gets and may want to hurt someone. That anger can create bitterness in the heart against even innocent ones such as the individual's own child. When anger turns to bitterness, it causes emotional pain. It means that focus is on the hurt [incident] and the person who caused it. Since some situations are the result of inconsiderate verbal exchanges or physical hurts, this could have happened earlier in life.

Some children harbour grief and pain from molestation, and manifest their hurt in their adulthood. They do this when they become angry and uncontrollable even in the presence of someone kind because they feel safer that the individual might not react the way a parent would have done in childhood. Counselee's have been very vocal and angry in sessions, forgetting that I am there to help and not to harm. During such times, I had to remain discreet, prayerful and calm until the rage died down. Although the individual knows that the object of his or her outburst does not deserve it, there seems to be no fear of expressing feelings.

For example, a husband will vent on his dutiful and loving wife. Emotional pain makes the individual focus on the self; rather than thinking about the persons, he is hurting with his angry outbursts. It becomes a selfish attitude and a time of self-preservation.

In the case of the parent and child relationship, adults have reported how unpleasant a parent was to them. In one situation, a mother did nothing to encourage or enhance one of her children's education experiences. Even as an adult she has not shown a modicum of interest concerning the accomplishments of her child now an adult.

According to Semands (1993) "One of the most common parental family situations which produces perfectionism and depression is unpleasantable parents. Such parents give only conditional love which demands that certain standards are lived up …" p.78. This might work in some situations, but cannot be generalized. There are children who have been successful, but the parent paid no attention or gave no encouragement to the child.

The inference is that it depends on the parent's interests, personality, and the relationship exhibits towards the child. There are two main situations which might be the result of emotional pain, and they are passive aggressive behaviours and anger.

Passive Aggressive Behaviour

The passive aggressive individual displays this behaviour in his interpersonal relationships. This can be with manager and employee; parent to child; pastor and members and vice versa. The demonstration is subtle, yet mixed with aggression and malice.

The person may not express himself openly, but beneath the surface, he is angry and waiting for the right moment to use innuendoes with insulting remarks to make his voice heard. He can appear friendly, and to be reliable. However, that person only waits for an occasion to strike with verbal assaults.

Another point is that the individual will be a procrastinator, and does not care if he is late or if duties are done. There is hostility and animosity with the use of jokes to get his feelings across, while the person does not care who gets hurt. He is stubborn and resentful of others.

A father who has to pay child support may seek every opportunity not to pay on time or to limit his interaction with the child if he thinks the mother was unfair to take him to court to support his child.

The teen who believes a parent is unfair may show aggression in subtle ways to impede and cause the parent aggravation. There are many ways in which an individual will display passive aggressive behaviours.

Anger

Anger is an emotion which sometimes cause fear to those who are around the angry person. Sometimes individuals are angry about disappointments, past mistakes, and failures.

According to Anderson, Zuehlke and Zuehlke (2002), "The victims of abuse may project their anger on to others around them" (p.251). As mentioned earlier, there were times in the counseling sessions when a counselee would get extremely angry with outbursts of "What was I supposed to do. I did not know he would have hurt me. I thought he loved me," in relation to a romantic affair which went wrong.

However, when an adult remember abuses from parents, looking back he knows it was a dreadful thing which he could do nothing about at the time. It is the memory and the lack of support then, which will make him become volatile and expressive if he thinks the effect of the abuses is an irreversible damage to his self-esteem, development, and life. He will be even angrier if there have been multiple failures such as faulty investments, broken marriages and other disappointing situations. The individual may become hostile even to a spouse who had nothing to do with the past.

One could theorize that men who abuse their spouses could be projecting their anger from a cold and insensitive mother who abandoned them as a child. Most men will not talk about an abusive childhood, but would rather subject themselves to over excess with substances such as drugs, alcohol or sex to deaden the pain in their hearts. Everyone needs love and especially as a child.

Emotional Fire Wall

Painful emotions hurt very deeply and can be a struggle to overcome or even to heal. In some situations, despite the intake of sophisticated medications and the most skilful therapeutic interventions, the response is either minimal or non-effective because the individual has built up an emotional fire wall impenetrable from the outside. This is a mechanism to protect the self from being hurt, since he or she no longer trust others and in extreme cases, has lost the reality to life.

The wall is so well-built that no one, despite how compassionate the intention, will be able to break through unless the hurting gives permission and approves of the individual that he or she is trustworthy. Outside of this authorization, the opportunity for entrance into that person's life is virtually impossible.

The reason for the emotional fire wall is to keep secrets of the past to which the individual is attached, and has become a prisoner. The past turned out to be a fortress, because there is a need for answers which the individual believes can only come from the experiences of childhood.

No one should try to break down the emotional fire wall because such an attempt might only create fear and distrust. It takes time and careful reasoning with wisdom to enter that person's life.

Keep in mind that childhood hurts are real and they do visit the individual as an adult. Not many are able to overcome and move on successfully. The ones who are behind the emotional fire wall have not been able to cope with past hurts, and for this reason it will take sincere and well-meaning intervention with trust and confidentiality to help such an individual.

G

Depression
Nobody cares about me!

- *Why do I feel so hollow, sad, alone and despondent? I try to be happy but it is such a struggle even though I have many good things going for me.*

- *Should I tell someone how I feel?*

- *I just hate myself.*

- *Why is life so unfair to me?*

- *Where is God?*

- *Does God love me?*

What is Depression?

From a spiritual view depression is a type of spirit conceived in the *thoughts*, expressed in the *emotions*, and displayed in *behaviour*.

Depression is both a mental and spiritual sickness, which attacks many people and for some, it has become clinical whereby medical intervention is necessary. Some types of depression turn out to be temporary, while others are seasonal.

Other points about depression

1. It is a spirit which can lead to debilitating results. People do not willingly admit to how they feel because from the exterior they have no reason to feel dejected. They have no reason to be sad, yet they are.

2. Depression is anger turned on the inside. There are times in our lives when we have been disappointed, or treated unfairly; but we do nothing about the way we feel. Instead, we turn our feelings on the inside. Suddenly, something happens bringing the old painful situations to the surface. Maybe the individual cannot do anything about what took place because it is too late. In some situations, it could be that the statutory time of limitations is gone and there is regret for not doing something then, but it is now too late. However, if you spend time fretting and telling yourself *if I had done this or that, I should have, I could have…*you are setting yourself up for pain. You are only enlarging and deepening your wounds.

3. Depression torments an individual, similar to the negative emotion of fear because it brings him or her to a state of hopelessness, and helplessness.

4. Depression traps its victims in a tunnel filled with *misery, gloom, desolation, anguish, heartache, guilt, regret*, and *sorrow*. The victim isolates himself from loved ones, and those who can help and give support to move out of the gloom and despair.

Identifying Depression

Depression is an emotional feeling. You might rise one morning feeling ecstatic and in a cheerful mood. Unexpectedly, for no apparent reason you find the mood gradually begins to decline and a cloud covers you. This might last hours or even days. If you do not capture it and deal with it immediately, you will suffer. If you feed into it, it will clasp your mind like a snake.

Everyone suffering from depression may not respond the same way. According to Kottler & Brown (1992), "Even though there are maybe a dozen major problems that frequently present themselves to a counselor, there are endless variations on those themes...the counselor should understand the problem thoroughly and have had some experience in handling it" p.8.

This is an extremely significant point which every counselor should note since it would be impossible to help someone suffering from depression if there has been no former knowledge about the condition.

Depression cannot be dealt with in an off-handed manner by telling the person he or she will get over it or that what happened to the individual is common to everyone. In my experience I have heard of therapists only receiving the fee, writing a prescription, or just asking, "How was your week?" This is like giving a band aid [first-aid] followed by setting the next appointment.

Along with knowledge on how to treat the depressed, the counselor must be very patient and empathetic. The person did not become depressed on the way to the office. Something happened in that person's world to have brought him or her to the office seeking help.

The truth about depression is that it is a soul sickness requiring delicate intervention. Although there are medications to calm the individual and to give some relief, those things cannot cure the sickness of the soul.

Depression: Sickness of the Soul

We are tripartite beings with spirit, soul, and body. If any of these structures is out of order it will affect the entire body. Each one though individual, is dependent on the other for mental and spiritual balance.

No one can see the soul which, like the spirit, is immaterial. It must be made clear that sickness of the soul cannot be diagnosed with a stethoscope. It is not easily identifiable such as when there is a bruise on the body. When we are sick, we feel pain and seek for comfort.

However, with the soul the sickness is not easily recognizable because the root is deeply embedded. Nevertheless, if unforgiveness is the cause for the depression it will block the individual from interacting with others, and isolate him or her. Social isolation can be painful even when caused by the individual.

Therefore, it is the responsibility of the hurting individual to express feelings in precise language so that the therapist will be able to help. Moreover, "When the burden is a weight on the soul instead of a weight on the body, it must be shared by the heart rather than the hands" (Tan & Ortberg, 1995) p.62.

Undoubtedly, soul problems are deep and need someone who has the time and empathy to listen and to render the kind of assistance needed. In some situations the counselee may come and only speak of superficial incidences.

Yet, the major problem may not be mentioned unless the therapist is experienced to notice by the attitude and mannerisms that there are other underlying anxieties.

Since we cannot see or touch the soul, when it suffers with emotional pain the individual retreats into an invisible familiar cave to find comfort and solace.

She sways in the darkness of depression alone and isolated from those who are ready to help and give support. The gate is closed, as the individual trembles in the quietness.

Sometimes we wonder why people become depressed and hide within themselves with food, drink, work, sex, drugs or anything to comfort the aching soul.

Although supporters will use all kinds of creative events to coax the individual to be more interactive, they do not always work.

Depression is a soul pain when the emotions are over-charged with cares, or the individual is incapable of managing the onslaught of bad memories of the past fueled by new painful events.

Soul pain cannot be seen by the naked eye; it requires spiritual discernment to arrive at a significant diagnosis in order to help the person suffering.

The soul pain will affect the body which responds with other problems which might be psychosomatic, physical, and of course behavioural. Individuals become angry, they break relationships, and will cry at the least bit of unusual event or disappointment.

Why do people become so depressed that they hide within themselves? Why do children conceal their emotional pain in childhood, and later display the hurts in behavioural problems to their spouses, and work colleagues.

When childhood incidents are played out in adulthood this could be unforgiveness which often traps someone into bondage and bitterness.

The child may decide that the parents were who too harsh, unkind, mean, and insensitive. For these reasons some adults have difficulty forgiving parents and moving on with their lives. They become trapped in depression which might become chronic.

Whatever the reasons for depression, it must not be ignored. The individual must recognize the changes in his or her life and watch the thought pattern.

Many times it is the disappointment of being unable to put up a defense during childhood, which will make the individual sink into depression thinking it is too late to do something about the hurts.

It may be too late to defend oneself against an angry parent, but is it ever too late to seek help? Is it ever too late to help oneself to move on to a happier life by letting go of past hurts?

There is always someone who cares whom we can trust with our confidences, who is patient, kind and understanding; someone who will not judge us or cast blame for holding out so long.

Someone might refer to the trials of Job [2] and his depression, yet fails to understand that he had to face himself and accept the fact that while God may seem to have been testing him, he had faults. No one is without faults, even a child who was abused by a parent.

Since we all have personalities different from one another, we will hurt others consciously and unconsciously. For Job, until he was confronted by God about his faults, he was then able to come of his cave of complaining, and admit that God is righteous in all that He does.

Self-Destruction

The depressed individual must seek help in a timely fashion otherwise, if he or she remains in this mode it might lead to self-destruction. If the individual cannot find answers to his life the outcome might be destructive through various forms of substances, careless living and so many other outcomes.

The person who is emotionally healthy will use these substances with moderation, the unhealthy person might use them as crutches or safe havens in which to hide their pain.

The depressed might try to overcome the feelings with some type of lighthearted inconsequential behaviour to escape the badgering of his soul for which he cannot find a cure. He has not shared his feelings with those who might be able to help, and refuses to involve them because he does not want to be a bother.

What makes matters worse is that all therapists are not equal. While there are those who take the time to go to the heart of the matter, others only treat symptoms even up ten years with only medication and inappropriate treatments not compatible with the problem.

---

[2] See the book of Job

Those persons response is to write a prescription relating to what is superficial; but the real problems remain untouched because of course, this takes time.

During this time of professional negligence the hurting person continues to sink deeper each day, until he makes a decision from which he might not return.

He sees only losses and failures and unable to find answers or reasons for life's circumstances which seem to be overwhelming and frustrating.

He combines his hurts and pains from childhood with present situations; maybe a lost job, failed marriage or anything which is close to him and might consider life a disappointment. For that individual each impediment is catastrophic, and maybe he tries to resolve problems but fails.

These are the situations which will hammer at this mind causing more stress and feelings of despair.

Depression must not be viewed lightly. Instead, it must be considered a disease as any other, but this can become dangerous when it progresses and reaches the depth of the soul making the individual repress his feelings until something happens in life to revive and reinstate everything.

An assumption here is that childhood emotional abuse may remain latent if the individual finds other sources of interest to take his mind from those hurts. He might have a happy family, successes and great accomplishments, and is able to overcome those hurtful past.

Someone in this position is better able to deal with childhood hurts successfully and move on with life.

It is the individual who has had successive failures in relationships, business, financial distresses and so many other incidents which will certainly impact the response he gives to life-changing circumstances.

Some Causes for Depression

No one is exempt from the condition of depression because it is not something any person can take an immunization against. It can affect just anyone at any time and the causes are numerous from the side effects to some medication, to personal losses and disappointments. It is possible to be depressed after a successful experience, for no apparent reason. Some depressions are uneventful, and other cause could be from lack of faith in God. This happens when our faith fails, and we begin to doubt His mercies, grace, and love.

Many Christians can relate to the dry season and feelings of abandonment by God. The ministry can become depressing when there are financial difficulties, sicknesses, loneliness, betrayal, abuse, rejection, and persecution. One of the weaknesses or maybe signs is that the depressed person will withdraw from family and even interests.

Life-Changing Events
Depression can be the result of disappointment from life-changing events such as death, divorce, separation, singleness, unemployment; losses from natural disasters such as storms, fires, accidents and so on. Facing change is a risky situation. It means leaving the known for the unknown, the familiar to the unfamiliar. There is always some measure of fear, anxiety, and distress. There will be resistance to accept the new, after being comfortable with what used to be.

However, all change does not necessarily mean the result of failure, or that you deserve the misfortunes of life. We do not know why things happen, but when they do, it is an opportunity to use what we have in order to move on with life.

You may say "But I do not have anything left to move on." Nevertheless, if you looked deep within yourself, you will be surprised to find that there are untapped resources. You will find innate abilities waiting to evolve.

Why not face the challenges of your misfortune by looking *within* for some dream, hope, goal, which you have put aside over the years. Look deep within yourself and ask yourself "What can I do at this stage of my life?" "How can I change this situation to something that will benefit me and my family?"

Has this disaster caused you to become addicted to substances, which you were not involved in before? This is what sudden change does to some people and will lead them into depression. For you to successfully deal with change it requires a combination of *renovation, restoration*, and *transformation*.

1. *Renovation* – <u>renewal</u> of your mind, <u>repair</u> of damaged emotions, <u>reconstruction</u> of your life;

2. *Restoration* – dealing with grudges and resentment by making amends – forgiveness; restitution – replace; reinstatement;

3. *Transformation* – makeover; alteration of lifestyle; change your way of thinking; and doing things which make you happy.

All those concepts are echoing – *change*

Diseases

Depression can be the result of certain diseases such as lupus, hepatitis, AIDS, cancer, Parkinson's, and side effects from some drugs.

Physical Problems

Over-work, lack of sleep, vehicular accidents, and change in sexuality from diseases, fatigue, and other physical conditions can result in depression. Some of those situations I would term *self-imposed depression* because our bodies do talk to us, and if we do not listen, we tire out ourselves and pay later for our lack of discretion. What kind of physical problems do you have? Have you received help for those problems? What are you doing to make things better in order to improve your health?

Negative thoughts

Have you reconciled your thoughts concerning the losses you suffered, in terms of who is to blame, those who did not help you, and who caused the disappointment? It is important to pay attention to your thoughts.

Beliefs and Values

Have you lost your beliefs and values because of a disaster? You need God in all of your life despite the disappointments and unmet desires. Where are you now?

Unhealthy Emotions

Any unhealthy emotions can lead to depression. There are times when we harbour certain *must* beliefs. I *must* achieve certain goals by the time I am 35 years of age. I *must* have a child by the time I am 25. I *must* be married by the time I am 30 something. If we place certain demands on ourselves, which we fail to accomplish, this can lead to depression and when we do not accept failure and disappointments as advantages to move on to something else. Many people cannot handle disappointments as learning experiences and for this reason, they take every skewed event as the end of their life.

Grief

This is an emotion we must deal with when we come face to face with it. We should not ignore grief because this might lead to other serious situations. Still, we should not spend the remainder of our lives grieving over any situation. Not many people can go through grief with some measure of smoothness. For some, there is *denial* of the facts; *anger* because it happened to them, *depression* and of course *sadness* because of the loss; *guilt* because you could or could not do anything about the disaster; *acceptance* when you accept the positive memories and the fact that you can do nothing about the event. The quality of your emotional health is vital to accepting change. *Do not pretend, or deny the truth of your losses.*

Fear and Anxiety

There are many conditions which will cause fear. In childhood it could be the absence or intermittent visits of a parent. The child whose hopes of having a steady relationship with a parent will become distraught, with feelings of abandonment if the parent does not visit him within a certain period of time. Eventually, he grows up thinking everyone will abandon him as the parent did. Moreover, we become fearful and anxious when our lives take sudden changes. Usually the next move is to avoid and run, in order to escape. You must deal with fear; otherwise, it will cause torment and keep you in bondage.

Unfulfilled Needs

Childhood hurts can re-surface when something catastrophic happens in an individual's life which changes the entire structure. Fear may keep that person from seeking help. Despite the fears the individual must begin to think about what he needs to help him move from where he is to another level in life. What are your desires?

Some Preliminaries for the Depressed

- Acknowledge that you are depressed and describe your feelings.
- Acknowledge that you need help and cannot fight this alone, especially if situations do not change quickly.
- When did you first start feeling depressed? What do you think brought it on?
- Be very precise in your description, and do not leave out anything. Give details of events, people, and your feelings.
- Did something happen at work or church, in your finance; or health?
- Were you on any medication?
- What is your relationship with the Lord? Do you pray or attend church often?

Healing from Depression

Depression is an enemy to *spiritual progress*, *social* and *interpersonal* life. When you are depressed, you seek for isolation. You do not want to talk with anyone, and at times, you do not want to eat. In fact, life seems more like an enemy to you than a friend.

One could infer that many people take their lives because they are in that deep dark hole of despair. It is a dismal tunnel of horror, which is impersonal, lonely, and seductive. The enemy tells his victims that life is uselessness, and there is no way out.

However, there is a way out of depression. If you have been honest in your answers concerning past and present events, here are a few ideas for moving from depression into God's wonderful peace and contentment.

1. I know it is hard to pray, but pray, even if all you say is "Lord I am here again, please help me" [Psalm 20].
2. God will give you peace when you tell Him your cares [Philippians 4:6-7].
3. Have faith in God [Hebrews 11:6]. Believe that He loves you [John 3:16].
4. Take God at His word and put your complete trust in Him [Proverbs 3:5-6].
5. Do not isolate yourself from family, church, or friends.

6. Change your thought pattern, and this will help you to control your emotions and your behaviour [Philippians 4:8].

7. Saturate you mind with the word of God. Let them come through your pores [Colossians 2:16].

8. Speak words of life and not death. I mean, do not speak negatively about your situation. Speak positive language that will bring death to *negative, irrational*, and *distorted* thinking [Proverbs 18:21].

9. Hope in God and do not doubt His love [Psalm 42, 43].

10. Believe that God's desire is to do you good and not evil [Jeremiah 29:11].

11. Take time to meditate on God's words, and sing songs of praise unto Him [Ephesians 5:19, Colossians 3:16].

12. Talk with God, confess your sins, and turn away from them [1 John 1:8-9].

13. Speak to the spirit of depression as you would to an infertile tree you want to bear or against any mountain in your life [Mark 11].

14. Keep your heart in the right place [Proverbs 4:23].

15. Develop a strong emotional health by confessing the truth of God's word from your heart [Romans 10:8].

16. Pay attention to what goes into your mind, and what you imagine in your quiet time [1 Corinthians 10:4-5].

17. Never lose hope in God. He does not fail [Proverbs 3:5, 6].

18. Know who you are in God [1 Peter 2:9].

19. Put on the whole armour of God [Ephesians 6:12-18].

Other Psychological Effects

With verbal abuse, it is possible that the child may grow to forget and the pain may not be as sharp in adulthood. Sexual abuse will always have a lasting effect and be a life-sentence for the child from which he or she may have that constant reminder. For some women when they become married there may be difficulties trying to overcome the memory of those situations.

Someone related that his wife was not responding to his advances and could not tell why this was happening. She seemed moody and unresponsive at times. After asking a few questions he shared that she had been molested as a child. He was encouraged to go with her to therapy in an attempt to help her overcome the traumatic experience which has haunted her life and affected their marriage.

Clearly although a victim might get over physical and verbal assaults, with sexual abuse it will be the most difficult to overcome. Usually with sexual abuses the child is terrified with threats if he or says anything to an adult.

Therefore, even though the child finds the encounters intolerable, fear will keep the "little secret" from getting out. Despite the discomfort, shame and embarrassment the child will not talk about the assaults. Even in some homes where the behaviour is prevalent in generations, it must be held in confidence.

Sometimes grandmother, mother, daughter and granddaughter were victims of sexual assaults from a male in the family. There are cases where the grandfather was father to the daughter's child. He then becomes the father and grandfather.

For many victims they do not have the courage to report incidences after leaving home. A few might bring it out into the open, while others keep quiet accepting the probability that the statute of limitation has passed.

The long-term effect from sexual abuses is depression which is a sickness needing professional intervention. Depression may lead to isolation whereby the individual does not interact or socialize because he or she feels dirty and unworthy.

In some cases the person may end up hating the opposite gender and will choose his or her own gender for companionship. The woman may view males to be animals who only cause hurt, but do not love. The male may continue with the lifestyle in which he was brought.

Part 5

Healing from Childhood Emotional Abuse

The individual who is the victim of abuse must take steps to get healing otherwise tension builds up. When life-changing events occur, it is important for the individual to deal with the emotions by expressing feelings in order to gain relief. In contrast, maybe you are hurting so badly that you hide your feelings.

What you must Do

1. Healing begins with you.
2. You must want to be healed, and this begins in your mind [*thoughts*].
3. If your hurt is as bad as you think, then it is time to rid yourself of it.
4. Remove the mask, take a reality check and face yourself with the truth that you have been hurt, and you need help!
5. Do not hide behind the crutches anymore.
6. You are numb and cannot express so you hide your feelings on the inside.
7. In order to express your feelings you must identify and describe your feelings with descriptive language before you can manage your emotions.
8. What are you feeling right now?
9. Can you name the emotion?
10. When did you first notice it? For example, a feeling of fear will result in tightness of the body especially the throat, clenching of the fists, goose bumps, or sweating.

11. Next, examine your behaviour such as change in facial expressions, or the tone of your voice.

For example, someone might shout at you in the presence of others and you felt embarrassed. It is not the [shout] you will respond to, but it is the feeling of *embarrassment*.

Analysis: [*act*] event, [*cognitive*] interpretation, the [*affective*] emotional response, and this can lead to anger [*behaviour*].

A

29

Remove Emotional Contaminants

Emotional hurts are not fantasy or fairytales; they are real to the person who has experienced such painful situations. When someone complains of hurt whether fresh or from the past, no one should disparage the individual because he knows how painful the situation is to him.

However, despite the painful memory of hurts it is the duty of the person who is feeling the discomfort to seek for relief through self-talk, therapy or some means whereby he or she can be healed of the painful situation.

Emotional hurts will cause any person to harbour a variety of toxic elements which only make the situation worse for him.

Those contaminants include malice, hatred, anger, unforgiveness, low self-esteem, and blame, resentment, and constant complaining.

Until the individual purpose to change bad attitude towards the circumstances, rather than focus on them, there will always be discomfort in the heart and life.

Self-Examination

Ask yourself these questions, and take a moment to think about them:

- Why am I angry?
- Why do I feel this way?
- Did I contribute to this situation?
- What is my attitude towards this person, situation, God, or myself?
- Has God failed me?
- Who failed me?

Until you are able to *analyze* your feelings and *acknowledge* them, in order to *identify* the cause effectively for your *chronic emotional pain*, you will continue harbouring toxins in your system. By harbouring those toxins, you will continue to be *irrational* in your *thinking*, which leads to bad *attitudes* and *behavioural* problems.

You, have to make the Decision

- Do you need help?
- Do you need support?
- How will you go about changing those behaviours?
- Are you willing to change, or are you comfortable with them?
- To break certain old habits takes time for re-learning new ones.
- Are you ready for the change?

♦ If you desire in your mind to change, but still hold on to certain aspects of the circumstance, you will not realize and experience qualitative change. Change begins in your heart, with your thoughts.

Personal Decision for Change

It is a self-talk exercise. *You must purpose in your mind that:*

♦ I want to change.

♦ I am leaving those thoughts in the graveyard.

♦ I do not want them in my system anymore.

When faulty thoughts come to your mind say to yourself,

♦ I am not going there today.

♦ I will find something else to think about.

♦ I will think on something worthwhile, positive, and meaningful.

♦ Stop yourself at will.

1. However, you will need the Holy Spirit.

2. You need to pray each time those thoughts come into your mind.

3. You are the one who entertains them when they come.

4. Do not blame others for your thoughts.

5. Others may have contributed to your pain, but you have control over your *thoughts*, *attitudes* and *behaviour*.

6. If you are still in the same place where the situation is active, then you need to make changes to get yourself out of it.

Before making changes, ask yourself

- ◆ Who will be affected by this?

- ◆ What effect will this make in my life?

- ◆ What will be the consequences?

- ◆ How will the outcome improve my situation?

You might change from one place to the other, but you still take your thoughts with you.

Similar to how you would not let an intruder into your home, do likewise with emotional toxins.

B

Dealing with Emotional Toxins

Before you can be healed you must rid yourself of emotional toxins. Indeed, everyone has experienced some kind of disappointment and suffering in life. No one is immune to life-changing circumstances. They are the realities of life and no one can escape their intrusion.

The source of hurts, pains, disappointments come from various areas and situations. When those events take place, the heart is wounded, spirits are wounded, and emotions are traumatized. People face all kinds of emotional wounds and those wounds can be hidden secretly in the heart covered by anger, and expressed in anti-social behaviours.

In order for an individual to be free of emotional toxins, the first place to begin is the heart. Emotional toxins will keep the individual in the bondage of unforgiveness and emotional pain.

Identifying Toxins in the Heart

The toxins in the heart include hatred, malice, confusion, anger, fear, and an anxious spirit. The individual displays irritation, anger, loud outburst, rudeness, and difficulty.

Preparing your Heart

- *Heart Searching* – the Word through the Holy Spirit [Psalm 139:23-24, 19:14]
- *Heart Cleansing* – [Psalm 24:3-5, Psalm 51:10]
- *Heart Restructuring/Restoration* – [Psalm 51:10]
- *Identify* reasons for a holistic healthy life-style – body, soul, and spirit
- *Understand* why it is important to be flexible and less rigid with faulty beliefs
- *Identify* areas of faulty thinking habits
- *Examine* your thinking processes and understand how they interrelate with emotions, attitudes, and behaviour
- *Identify* cues that trigger faulty thinking – from past, and present experiences; or unrealistic desires for the future
- *Develop* and practice positive thinking habits

The Process for Cleansing

You must prepare to eradicate your heart from all manner of toxins, which include hurts from the past.

1. Recompense no man evil for evil [Romans 12:17a, 19]

2. Provide things honest in the sight of all men [Romans 12:17b]

3. Avoid vengeance, pay back or retaliation [Matthew 5:38-42]

4. Avoid slothfulness in business, do not be a procrastinator [Romans 12:11]

5. Bless and do not curse verbally, or in your heart [Romans 12:14]

6. Avoid long-standing anger [Ephesians 4:26]

7. Do not plan to do evil [Romans 13:10, 14]

8. Forgive quickly from your heart [Matthew 6:14, 15]

9. Renewing your thoughts [mind] [Philippians 4:8]

10. Control your emotions – *temperance* [Galatians 5:22,23]

11. Control your behaviour – [Ephesians 4:26-27]

Stop Worrying

1. "Take no thought for your life…" (Matthew 6:25-34). If you believe these words, then you should not worry about things especially when you cannot change them. Keep your trust in the Lord and wait patiently for Him to act on your behalf.

2. "Therefore all things whatsoever ye would that men should do to you, do ye even so to them…" (Matthew 7:12). You will only receive what you have given out.

3. If you forgive, you will be forgiven (Matthew 6:14). God is fair and just in all His ways. Therefore, if you require someone to forgive you, then you must do the same.

4. Demonstrate what you believe and be consistent (James 1:22). Do not pretend.

If you have faith, doing will be more than wishing or talk. You must purpose in your heart that you need change, cleansing, a new life. For this to take place with effect, there will be evidence that you have made a new start concerning your plans for the rest of your life.

Believing in God and knowing about Him is not enough. Saying that you have faith will not be enough. It takes a decisive effort to read the word and accept what it says. James 1:22 is actually stating that you must listen to the word, have knowledge about what you read, and then do what it says:

1. *Listen* to the word – being attentive
2. *Knowledge* of the word – understanding, interpreting
3. *Taking action* – doing the word, acting upon what you heard

E

Forgiveness

One of the hardest things to do when we have been hurt is to forgive. This gets even more difficult when the hurt comes from someone close who might have deceived and abused us. Nevertheless, we must obey the Scriptures that if we do not forgive, we will not be forgiven [**Matthew 6:14-15**]. There are people who have gone to the doctor with complaints, which he cannot diagnose because the problem is unforgiveness.

Doris had parents who were insensitive and distant. Her father was extremely stern and did not appreciate his children from her recollection. They were kept in order with the necessary things, but one thing was needed and it was his love for her and her siblings.

During her growing up years to adulthood neither she nor her siblings had any close contact with dad or even mom. They were the type of parents who did what was necessary, but would not include the necessities with expressions of love.

As she grew, went to college, carved out a career, married and had children she still felt the loss of her parents' love and held them in her heart.

In one of our sessions I asked the following questions:

1. *Have you forgiven your parents?*
2. *Can you forgive your parents?*
3. *How do you know you have forgiven them?*
4. *What evidence can you show to prove that you have forgiven them?*
5. *How do you feel about them now?*
6. *Do you have a relationship with them?*

Questions to Consider

1. Will the emotionally hurt individual forgive the parent?

2. Is it possible to forgive with so many painful memories of the past?

3. How does one forgive painful emotional situations?

In reflecting on the attitude and behaviour of some parents it might be easy to hold on to those painful memories. However, for the child this decision will not help him or her. The reason is that emotional pain is real and will erode self-confidence and social development.

The individual may decide to harbour every incident and event regardless of the nature and how long the incident took place. Despite the pains we suffer from parents, it is in the interest of the emotionally bruised to seek help and deliverance.

When Jonah objected to God's mercy on Nineveh, His response was *Thou hast had pity on the gourd, for which thou hast not laboured, neither made it grow; which came up in a night, and perished in a night. And should not I spare Nineveh, that great city, wherein are more than six score thousand persons that cannot discern between their right hand and their left hand; and also much cattle [Jonah 4:10-11].*

God's explanation for saving those people was not a defense, but sincere concern for a people who were out of His will, and whom He wanted to rescue.

We cannot compare God's reasoning with humans', but many parents who abused their children whether emotionally or physically were administering punishment or attitudes, which they themselves experienced as children, and which they thought was right. This does not mean to say that every parent is excused.

What is being conveyed is what caused a parent to hurt his or her own child? Since many were portraying and administering what they knew, then they must be excused. Still, how many fall into this category since so many issued abuse out of anger, hatred for a father; and not ignorance.

Forgiveness may be a long process, but it is necessary for the individual to move on and to be healed, and delivered from the past.

30

Lay Aside Childish Things

This chapter is not meant to minimize the effect of what the individual is experiencing. Furthermore, no one can comprehend the emotional pain, disappoint, and feeling of treachery from parents which an individual feels to cause him or her to be paralyzed with fear, doubt, mistrust, low self-esteem and other factors which keep him in bondage.

Rather the aim is to help the individual move forward by understanding that although the parents did wrong, he or she now has a life to live which can correct the injuries of the past that dislocated his or her hope for a happy childhood. The individual can now order the quality of life desired in a way which is comfortable and acceptable to bring reasonable peace and contentment.

If the emotionally injured continues to hold on to the past he or she will be trapped for life in an abyss of unforgiveness; but there is no need for this to happen.

The emotionally abused in childhood will grow up with many signs of immaturity. Although he or she may be chronologically mature: yet not socially, emotionally or psychologically fully developed.

The adult might still have a little child on the inside seeking for parental approval, love, admiration, and acceptance. These are the beehive emptiness on the inside which brings about dependency.

Being emotionally abused in childhood is a serious matter which must never be overlooked or taken for granted when someone is in any of those underdeveloped situations. Maybe you wonder why someone who might be successful cannot find peace, contentment, and happiness.

The reason is glaring, but not many people understand the behaviours of those persons. Instead, they are sometimes criticized. The fact is that rejection is an awful feeling because everyone needs unconditional love which, for many in childhood this necessity was denied. In some situations, purposely when a parent openly shows disdain for one child but loves others in the home.

Despite childhood rejection and so many other negative situations, each person is keeper of himself, and should not allow the past to hold him or her in bondage preventing effective growth and development. According to Paul, *When I was a child, I spoke as a child, I understood as a child, I thought as a child: but when I became a man, I put away childish things" [I Corinthians 13:11].*

There are three salient themes here which Paul related to childhood demeanour – I *spoke* as a child, I *understood* as a child, and I *thought* as a child.

When we think of children they speak in terms of the here and now when you make a promise to them. They expect that when a parent says I am leaving, but I shall return the child, depending on the age might expect the return to be at least next day. That child may not be able to comprehend and calculate time span.

What is most important is the desperation to have mom or dad around all the time. This is the reason why many are so disappointed when there is a divorce in the family. Separation is critical because the child cannot understand that he or she will still see dad or mom occasionally.

The desperation is having them both at home to enjoy *all* the time and when this does not happen there is despair and anxiety. Some children fall into depression and withdraw within themselves.

For a child who has been emotionally hurt stress and depression are the reinforcements on which to lean in order to cope with disappointment. He might take the pain to adulthood if there has not been adequate intervention.

Nevertheless, now that the individual has grown to be an adult, it is time to let go and live life freely and not become a slave to past hurtful childhood experiences. This does not mean cynicism, but there comes a time to move forward and make the necessary changes for a healthy emotional life.

Moreover, since we are tripartite beings – body, soul, and spirit whatever affects one aspect has a direct effect on the other. It is important to make changes which will result to a better life, instead of living in the past.

While there will be times of recollection which is inevitable, no one should hide into a cave of emptiness with the poisons of those lost years to control his or her life.

Everyone must try to redeem the self from those hurtful experiences by not allowing them to dictate how he or she should live. Consider the fact that you are no longer with a parent whom you had to please in order to gain approval.

You now have the opportunity to be a better parent to your children than your parents were to you. Bring them up according to moral and godly virtues with love and acceptance so that they will have a better past than you had.

Avoid visiting those bad behaviours and principles on them because it will only perpetuate the error of your parents with their parenting skills, which led you to where you are. It is never too late to begin to live and appreciate life.

Laying aside childish behaviours means just what it says: put them aside, start over and enter the process for healing so that you can be a whole person not holding on to the past. Your healing begins with first looking at yourself by doing an introspection of who you are, what you need, and where you want to go.

Self-examination is critical to your healing because very often there are destructive behaviours, and faulty thoughts which are more dangerous than even the past hurts. Those behaviours are the bolster which you hold on to for comfort. However, those defenses are not positive luxuries to bask in for the rest of your life or even momentarily.

Instead they only leave you in a worse condition than you were because the memories make you bitter and angry. If you become desperate and determined that you do not want to face the past to relieve yourself, and instead resort to destructive substances, then you will be going down a spiral staircase which makes you dizzy as you descend into darkness.

Lose the little child within and begin anew by learning how to enjoy what you have by letting go of the past. Accept the fact that everyone has a past, but each one is different. Yours is different, but there is no need to hold on to it since it is so painful and does not add to your enjoyment.

In fact, your past may be what made you successful because you felt that you had something to prove to mom or dad who put you down and even verbalized that, "you will not amount to anything good; you will be a loser." Think about it, you have proven them wrong that you are somebody, and that you are successful.

Make a distinction concerning what was, and what is: then and now, and move on leaving that little boy or girl behind.

You are no longer a child waiting for that approval and appreciation from mom or dad. You now have your own children to love and who love you in return. Accept the changes and the accomplishments you have made in life.

Indeed, *When you were a child, you <u>spoke</u> as a child, you <u>understood</u> as a child, you <u>thought</u> as a child: but now you are an adult, you put away childish things"* You are grown and now speak, act, and think, as an adult ought to do.

You may need help from a friend, pastor or therapist, but do not remain in your condition. Find someone who can help you, and with whom you can connect.

Change Faulty Behaviours

Since we are constantly learning, faulty behaviours of the past can hinder those which are conducive to a warm loving environment which will help future generations. However, this depends on the impact previous generations had on the present.

For example, if the present or third generation is more intelligent and had the opportunity to learn the skill of socialization and the importance of love and appreciation, there is hope for this new learning to take precedence over the old.

There are young couples who will say, *"I will not do the same to my children as my parents did to me."* Here we have a decisive <u>change in outlook</u> and a <u>break in inherited family</u> mistakes.

Nevertheless, when emotional hurts occur in childhood, it affects behaviour, and even personality. The child who was once outgoing and pleasant can change and become angry, rebellious and disrespectful. Those behaviours will not help you. Rather, they will destroy you if you do not change.

Break Harmful Soul Ties

All friends are not equal, and there are those which you may have to eliminate from your life. This does not necessarily means you will not talk with them anymore, but you must know the effect each one has on your life and whether it is helping or destroying you.

Build Healthy Relationships

Begin with yourself. Loving yourself before you can love others. It begins with this principle, *Thou shalt love thy neighbour as thyself [Mark 12:31a].*

Set Limitations

If you purpose in your mind that you want to start over then you must set parameters. If you leave yourself open for others to use and abuse you because you are needy, most certainly you will constantly be hurt.

1. Therefore you must set <u>boundaries</u>.
2. Next, you must have <u>standards</u> which will govern what you expect and require from a suitor.
3. Finally, you must know the <u>qualities</u> you are looking in a companion.

You do not want to make the same mistakes you made before which kept you in a needy position for others to abuse you.

Everyone will not treat you the way you desire, but someone will respect your standards and might also meet your expectations.

By setting standards, it show that you are strong and able to cope with life which maybe you were unable to do before because you were dependent on others to fill your needs by being compliant to their requirements.

Self-Examination

1. Acknowledge that you have been hurt and need help.

    a. What hurts you the most?

    b. What disappoints you the most?

    c. How does your present life relates to your past?

2. What is the most troublesome situation which you believe is hindering you from moving forward?

    a. For example, fear, feelings of being abandoned

    b. Low self-esteem and feelings of being inferior

    c. Rejection

    d. Fear of being alone

    e. Insecurity

3. The things you are doing and the people in your life at present, do they satisfy your desires?

4. Come to terms with the realities of life that we all get hurt by others even our closest friends or relatives.

5. Identify weaknesses and work through anger.

    a. Why are you angry?

    b. With whom are you angry?

6. Get rid of faulty thoughts and bring them under subjection, and do not allow them to trap you into fantasy.

7. Admit to faults and do not try to please everyone.

8. Do not make yourself vulnerable and then blame others for using you

9. Do not expect anyone outside of God to meet your needs

10. Leave the emotional cave where you hide in times when things go wrong with you

11. Take care of yourself and do not depend on others to do it for you

12. Try not to regress. Rather, get professional help to guide you into moving from the past and begin to live life to its fullest.

13. Do not allow the past to dictate your future

14. Make necessary changes, and do not blame your mistakes on the past

15. Allow the child in you to grow up and mature into an adult because you cannot go back to the past and re-live it in order to regain what you missed

16. Do not remain static. Accept that changes will come and meet them head on

Finding your Identity

1. Who am I? What am I? What do I need?

2. What am I willing to give?

3. Be careful of the types of friends you chose. Seek for reliability, value, principles, and quality.

4. Do not select a friend just for the sake of having someone, anyone in your life. It will not last because it would be for the wrong motive

5. Know the reasons for getting into a relationship

6. Do not settle for seconds. Instead always aim for the best

7. Do not doubt yourself or compare yourself with anyone else

8. Do not allow men to use you for your body.

9. Your relationship must be for *love* and *satisfaction*. When those are missing it will be useless.

10. Develop ethical codes to govern your way of life and the choice of friends in your life

11. Do not make yourself vulnerable for others to use you.

12. Do not isolate yourself from life.

13. You must go after what you need with wisdom and understanding.

14. Decide what you need, from whom, and how you will achieve your desire.

15. Learn to encourage yourself no matter how alone you may feel. If you try you will be able to live with yourself without seeking out others to fulfill your needs.

16. Do not give up on yourself and do not listen to the voice which will tells you that you are loser. ***No child of God is a loser***.

Maintaining your Freedom

1. When you know that you have been freed from those pains, hurts, and the emotional wounds, stay free [Galatians 5:1].

2. Do not allow the past to dictate to you [Romans 8:1]

3. Let the word of God be your guide [Psalm 119:11]

4. Be careful of the friends you keep. Seek out those who are positive and Godly.

5. Change any negative attitudes you have harboured against God, the person who hurt you, yourself, and the world.

6. Take charge of your emotions and do not allow them to control you.

7. Maintain fellowship with other Believers.

8. Read inspirational books.

9. Be careful of the types of programs you watch on the television.

10. Maintain a strong and consistent prayer life.

11. Meditate on positive and spiritual things.

C

Managing Your Emotions

We are complex beings of body, soul, and spirit with needs and desires which require our attention. Within those systems we will find three domains the <u>cognitive</u>: <u>affective</u>, and <u>behavioural</u>. The **cognitive** deals with imaginations, thoughts, values, and more; the **affective** refers to moods, attitudes, and emotions; while the **behavioural** represents actions.

Emotions are part of our natural make-up and they influence our attitudes and behaviours. Each person is made of a full complement of emotions, which are powerful manifestations of our personalities and how we express ourselves in a given situation. They are symbols of communication we use to express dissatisfaction, or pleasantness. We use body language to express ourselves – raising the eyebrows, grin, frown, shrugging of the shoulders, slouching, and so on.

When we are hurt, we feel some type of emotion expressed in signals or symbols to tell us or someone that we are not pleased by the event. If a parent abuses a child physically or emotionally he might cry, shout, throw a tantrum or behave in a manner to show disgust. This behaviour might lead to even more severe abuses. Therefore, the child might decide to hold in his feelings fearing that by expressing them it will only escalate the parent's anger.

There are times when our emotions are out of control and we lash out at others who do not deserve our outbursts of temper. Tiredness, fear, anxiety, and stress will make us say the wrong things to those who are often trying to help us.

Usually, when we think over our actions we discover there was no justification for our behaviour. I believe everyone has done this sometime in life. You said the wrong thing or became angry with someone who simply asked a question. Parents do become angry when under stress and some of them hurt their children and might show some regret later. However, it is when there is no acceptance of hurting a child which will make him distressed.

Despite all this, when we become adults we must own our emotions. It is important to be in tune with our feelings and express them in a *controlled*, yet *assertive* manner. In order to control we must recognize the symbols and the signals our emotions send before we explode on someone who does not deserve our outbursts.

No one can deny the fact of childhood hurts if this is the case, but each person must know how to deal with those past situations so that they do not dictate how the rest of our life will be. The past is the past, and we must let go and move on to something better especially when we can see success and accomplishments in our lives.

Recalling a very successful couple, who came to me a few years ago. Both were in professional jobs, but there was a missing link. One spouse held on to the past and could not let go to move on.

The communication style was patterned in relation to the parental control of one to the other which the person inherited and was using it to rule and govern the spouse. It caused untold misery and much contention with constant threats of separation. What the individual forgot was that the parents' marriage did not last, and this one was heading in the same direction

Lack of control of emotions will cause problems and break relationships. If the hurt individual does not pay attention to what comes from the heart, that person will experience more pain, the end of which will make him or her feel that all men/women are bad.

Childhood hurts are real, but it makes no sense trying to correct the past by being obnoxious to innocent people such as a spouse or one's own children who had nothing to do with the past.

Let us look at Proverbs 4:23-26, where the writer talks about symbols of communication through emotions.

- *Keep thy heart with all diligence: for out of it are the issues of life.* Pay attention to your thoughts.
- *Put away from thee a forward [deceitful] mouth, and perverse lips put far from thee.* Be true to yourself.
- *Let thine eyes look right on, and let thine eyelids look straight before thee.* Trust in God and do not doubt His word.
- *Ponder the path of thy feet, and let all thy ways be established.* Make right decisions. Think before you speak, and be realistic.

1. It is important to think before you speak. If you blurt out everything you might later regret your actions. Although you were hurt in your childhood there is no excuse to destroy your life or cause distress for others who are in your life.

2. While you were a child you could not help yourself nor could you force your parents to love you or treat you right. You now have the opportunity to help yourself and to be the person whom you can be without their objections or rejection. You must learn to love yourself by changing your thought pattern.

3. Be careful of what goes into your mind and what you hold on to from your past. If the memory serves no valuable purpose, then you should let it go, otherwise it will become destructive and will also affect those around you.

4. Do not think that everyone ought to accept or like you; this would be impossible to expect. Nevertheless, you must know how to conduct yourself to prevent some incidents which may have been a hindrance in your relationships causing you to have many disappointments. Sometimes a hasty word, impatience, and being aggressive to make up for your past will only place you in a worse situation than when you were a child.

5. Maybe you could look back and ask yourself if you expected too much from your parents. What part did you play in the abuse you received from them? Since no one is perfect, we must acknowledge that we too make mistakes and expect others to overlook our faults. Therefore, we should be able to overlook the things parents' have done to us especially if they did not do so out of spite.

D

Monitoring Emotions

When we slip and say the wrong thing it seems so easy to say "sorry" whether we mean it or not. Still, how often can we say sorry to the same person after repeating the same mistakes?

We control our emotions by controlling our thoughts.

Philippians 4:8 "*Whatsoever things are true, whatsoever things (are) honest, whatsoever things (are) just, whatsoever things (are) pure, whatsoever things (are) lovely, whatsoever things (are) of good report; if (there be) any virtue, and if (there be) any praise, think on these things.*"

Although it might be difficult to control our emotions at all times, yet, we can "change how we think and we can choose what we believe" Anderson, Zuehlke & Zuehlke (2000), p.105.

The message from Paul is actually saying we are to consider what comes into our minds and do an exercise of elimination so that we can experience the peace of mind we all need.

The person who was abused as a child can decide what he will allow to control his thought pattern from those past episodes in his life. What will he focus on and what needs to be rid of?

It may seem difficult to control emotions at all times. However, there are many devices which will help us in managing the way we respond to unfavourable situations and objectionable people in our lives. We have caller ID's on the phone.

We can send emails, if it is better than confrontation to avoid getting angry. Even in the email we have time to read and re-read so that the language is not as harsh as it might have been if the individual was present.

Another way is to delay response until we know that we can control our emotions. The worst thing would be to respond in anger.

Parents who do not control their emotions will express themselves in anger with shouting, threats, punishments and a myriad of situations to make the child "pay."

Nevertheless, it is better to walk away and calm yourself rather than spill angry lava in the environment to infect those who are nearby.

Someone might become comfortable with holding on to the hurts of the past. The individual may use the incidents as a comfort zone in which to hide because he believes he has a right to feel pain and to act in whatever manner he chooses.

Still, by holding on to the past can be the direct reason for the individual's emotional pain and not the incident which took place maybe decades. It is as if the individual wants to validate his hurt by holding on as his right.

Unexpressed Emotions

Those who do not show any emotions, no matter what happens, yet, they are hurting might well be the ones who will hurt you secretly. They are people numb to insults, and rebuke and can be described as passive aggressive.

They do not show any emotions or become easily worked up. For example, take the husband whom you think puts up with your nagging, and says nothing.

One day he might just walks out on you without notice. Pay special attention to those persons who do not show emotions – they can be very dangerous, so can the one who vents all the time.

Responses to Emotions

We respond according to our *beliefs*, *values*, *expectations*, *culture*, *personalities*, and *understanding* of a situation. These all influence our <u>evaluations</u> and <u>performance</u>. It is important to value your emotions, i.e. acknowledge them.

They are part of your life, do not ignore, but express them in the right manner, and do not allow them to control you.

Many relationships have been broken because someone did not control the tongue, which is the most vehement instrument for damaging interpersonal relationships.

The tongue is an instrument that speaks life or death depending on our thoughts and the value we give to an event and the emergent emotion. People often pay the price when the tongue is not controlled [*Proverbs 18:21*].

Keep in mind that the tongue is one of the most powerful organs in the human body which influences our intentions and feelings through words [*James 3*].

Feelings are important, but you must know how to respond to unjust situations with *dignity* and *character*.

If we are not careful, we will allow feelings to control our behaviour. We must take control and recognize that feelings can be very deceptive and are not always accurate.

Emotions and Past Events

Present emotions could be the product of events related to the past. Someone deceived you, and you are still holding feelings of regret and sadness. A family member or a friend died and you are suffering the loss.

Past events can hold us in bondage, therefore we must let go and move on since we cannot alter what took place.

Julie stated that each time she had a relationship disappointment she finds herself going back to the days of childhood.

It is as if she would retreat to her "safety cave" by hiding from the emotional pain. Another person finds that over-eating is her comfort while another felt at ease with drinking alcohol to numb the pain.

Emotions and Present Events

You received a promotion at work with an increment in pay and you are happy. You found the person of your dreams and you are elated, and in cloud nine. You have finally landed the job of your dreams, and you are happy.

Identifying Emotional Cues

There are times when it is better to analyze an <u>offensive event</u> before responding. Pay attention to the *thoughts* from the event, and the *emotions* resulting from the event and decide on a suitable *response*. Ask yourself a few questions.

Begin with some [I] statements before coming up with a reason or attacking another person.

This is where many misunderstandings take place because of impatience and lack of perception. Get facts, and information before making decisions.

1. Why do I feel this way?
2. Could it be that I am taking this thing out of context?
3. Did I say something to trigger this behaviour from…?

How do you react when someone *lies* on you, *insults* you, *shouts* at you, *deceives* you, or *ignores* you when you are talking? **Do you**

1. *Bottle* it up;
2. V*ent* immediately;
3. *Confront* at the right time; or
4. Keep a *record* for a future date.

Your Body: It is important to identify the cues, which trigger emotional outbursts. What brings about anger, irritability, frustration, or stress?

You might say "but I do not feel anything." Since our bodies experience most of our feelings, we need to check to find out if we are fearful about something.

If this is so, there will be a knot in your stomach. Your throat also might become tight, and these feelings will result in discomfort. You must know your body and be able to detect what is going on when an incident takes place.

Many people do not express outwardly, but they feel on the inside. Many are trapped by fear and for this reason are unable to express themselves.

Your Behaviour: Another cue is in behaviour. People will detect a change in our behaviour patterns. They will know that something is bothering us before we utter a word.

We express behaviours in our body language or what is called kinesics – such as gestures, shrugs or facial expressions.

Example, you meet your colleague or husband with a frown, that person will become curious about your well-being.

Types of Emotions

Emotions are feelings we experience after an event:

- *frustration* when we cannot understand certain things or event;
- *happy, joy, and love* when we trust and feel appreciated;
- *unforgiveness, malice, hatred* when we are offended;
- *rejection and loneliness* when we feel abandoned or when we have been hurt;
- *fear* when we feel terror;
- *anxiety* when we are impatient;
- *guilt and regret* when we have violated a value, principle, or belief;
- *disappointment* when someone disappoints us;
- *defeat* if we over-plan or over-estimate our expectations;
- *distress* when we are in despair and stressed out, or feel in adequate.

Processing a Response to an Event

Our *perception* of an event will evoke *emotions* resulting in either *negative* or *positive* *response*.

The reason is that we interpret events according to our perceptions and understanding of the event and the outcome plays a significant role in the type of emotional response to the event.

Each new and unrelated event is interpreted according to how it is perceived to happen. However, a new event that is related to a past event can influence the outcome and type of emotions that will be expressed. Some responses are spontaneous – sudden fright, or impulsive without thought.

Wrong thought patterns for interpreting incidents

1. *Overgeneralization* – not thinking clearly about the reason for a situation resulting in being over sensitive. Someone in this situation will make events seem worse than what they really are.

2. *Critical* – overlooking the good in one's life such as successes and accomplishments.
   Instead the individual sees only gray areas. One could even describe such as person as being pessimistic about life.

3. *Lack of Moderation* – there is no self-control. The individual goes overboard with situations, and believes he must complete everything even if it hurts.

4. *Self-deprecation* – after making a mistake the individual sees himself to be useless.

All those behaviours are the results of faulty thought patterns which can certainly keep the emotionally hurt individual in bondage.

31

Suggestions to Parents

1. Do not make the mistake of using the same methods from your parents to raise your children, even though it might seem to work, it might cause pain and distress to the entire family. While some ideas and aspects of inherited techniques may be transferred, parents must ensure that the type of discipline is necessary and warrants the offense.

2. Some grandparents believe harshness and corporal punishment to be the only means for obtaining obedience. Nevertheless, while it may be necessary to correct, it must be done in love and not because the parent has the right to do so.

3. Each parent must recognize that there are personality differences among their children. They should treat each child with adequate respect if they want to be respected. Parents should never forget that they are models which the children will imitate.

4. One of the greatest and most effectual methods for teaching is positive modelling with patterns of behaviour which will change a negative course to one that is effective and lasting.

5. Parents must reinforce good behaviour by acknowledging change and honour such effort by a child. It does not matter what the event might be. It could be improvement at school, treating a sibling better and so on. It is very important for a child to know that mother or daddy notices the effort he or she is making for improvement.

6. Some parents do not discipline children and if they do the standards and expectations are vague and in some cases impossible for a child to obey.

7. There are parents who not monitor the friends their children keep. This is a mistake.

8. Parents must supervise their children and censor some programs on the television which are not age appropriate for children to watch. This includes the internet and the type of music which comes in the home. Content of programs must be of educational and learning quality and of interest to hold the child's attention.

9. Some parents are tyrants rather than supportive to their children. They are brutal with harsh treatment.

10. Many parents believe that by giving a child everything he needs to win his love. This behaviour will eventually hurt the child when the parent cannot afford to give him what he wants.

11. Showing favouritism has one of the most destructive setbacks for a family. The one who suffers may leave home and never return. On the other hand the child who is idolized may not succeed the way the doting parent had visualized.

Conclusion

Everyone has some experience or event which took place in life which he or she wished never happened. What could be more desirable than having a happy and pleasant childhood, but not everyone has this wonderful blissful experience.

Many have suffered severely in every way possible such as physically, emotionally, psychologically, and spiritually – wondering where was God when all those terrible things took place.

God is always near, but He gives us wills and we decide what we will do, how, when, where and why we do the things we engage into.

Despite the fact that there are cruel people in the world, even among parents, relatives and friends, we cannot give up on life or ourselves.

There is always hope for change which can lead to a better life. Childhood emotional hurts are real and each person must know how to deal with those painful circumstances.

Pray for the parent or whoever caused the hurt and discomfort. This is the best way to walk away from emotional pain. It makes no sense holding on to grudges which only torments, cause mental strain, and bad attitudes.

Moreover, being resentful against a perpetrator only takes you into his or her space mentally. You will remain attached to the individual and the act of violence to you.

In addition resentment creates all kinds of emotional toxins which will make you physically sick. Forgive and move to a happy life.

Index

abandonment, - 163 -
adulthood, - 92 -
aggressive, - 37 -
Alcoholism, - 49 -
anger, - 67 -
Anger, - 120 -
angry, - 120 -
appreciation, - 21 -
Assertive, - 37 -
Barriers. *See* communication
behaviours, - 80 -
Biblical, - 97 -
boundaries, - 21 -, - 30 -, - 32 -, - 33 -, -
    46 -, - 63 -, - 246 -
Childhood, - 145 -
Childhood emotional abuses. *See*
    childhood abuses
closed environment, - 162 -
cognitive dissonance, - 175 -
Collaboration, - 60 -
commitment, - 111 -
communication, - 22 -, - 37 -, - 93 -, -
    165 -, - 227 -, *See* family
compassion, - 94 -
conflicts, - 22 -, - 35 -
corporal punishments, - 108 -
criticisms, - 36 -
criticizing, - 41 -
Culture, - 53 -
Dealing with Emotional Toxins, - 223 -
Definition of Emotions, - 141 -

demoralizing, - 144 -
Depression, - 126 -, - 199 -
Disagreements, - 49 -
Discipline, - 93 -
Discouraged, - 99 -
discouragement, - 49 -
disrespecting, - 41 -
divorce. *See* family
domestic violence. *See* family
drugs, - 118 -
Dysfunctional. *See* family
effect of childhood emotional abuse, -
    171 -
Emotional Abandonment, - 163 -
emotional abuse, - 130 -, - 157 -
Emotional Beehive, - 156 -
Emotional Contaminants, - 218 -
Emotional dependency, - 188 -
emotional holes, - 156 -
emotional neglect, - 144 -
Emotional Neglect, - 163 -
Emotional Pain, - 194 -
emotional paralysis, - 190 -
Emotional prostitution, - 173 -
emotional trauma, - 145 -, *See* domestic
    violence
emotional traumatic, - 63 -
emotional unit. *See* family
emotionally starved, - 174 -
environment, - 22 -
examples, - 88 -

Suggestions for further Reading

Anderson, N.T. Zuehlke, J.S. and Zuehlke T.E. (2000). *Christ Centered Therapy: The Practical Integration of Theology and Psychology*. Zondervan Publishing House

Balswick J.O. & Morland J.K. 91990). *Social Problems: A Christian Understanding and Response*. Baker Book House.

Craig, Grace J. (1996). *Human Development*, 7th. Ed. Prentice Hall

Eaker-Weil, B.E., & R. Winter. *Adultery, The Forgivable Sin -- Healing the Inherited Patterns of Betrayal in Your Family*. A Birch Lane Press Book Published by Carol Publishing Group, 1993.

Ekstrom, R.R., *How Media Influences Our Faith and Values: Media, Faith, & Families*. J. Roberto, ed. Don Bosco Multimedia, New Rochelle, NY, 1992.

Festinger, L. *A Theory of Cognitive Dissonance*. Stanford University, 1963.

Goldenberg I. & Goldenberg H. (1991). *Family Therapy*, 3rd. Ed. Brooks/Cole Publishing Company, Pacific Grove, CA

Kraft, C.H. (1993). *Deep Wounds: Deep Healing, Discovering the Vital Link between Spiritual Warfare and Inner Healing*. Servant Publications

Kottler, J.A. & Brown, R.W. (1992). Introduction to Therapeutic Counseling, 2nd Ed. Brooks/Cole Publishing, Company, CA

Lazarus, R.S. & Lazarus, B.N. (1994). Passion and Reason: Making Sense of Our Emotions. Oxford University Press.

Sarason G.I. and Sarason, B.R. (1996). *Abnormal Psychology: The Problem of Abnormal Behaviour,* 8th Ed. Prentice Hall.

Seamands, David A, (1993). *Healing your Heart of Painful Emotions*. SP Publications, Inc.

Tan, S-Y & Ortberg, Jr. (1995). *Understanding Depression: A Short-term Structured Model*. Baker Books

Vander Zanden, J.W. (1988). *The Social Experience: An Introduction to Sociology*. Random House.